First Book in Arithmetic

Frederic A. Adams

BIBLIOBAZAAR

FIRST BOOK

IN

ARITHMETIC:

COMPRISING

LESSONS IN NUMBER AND FORM.

FOR PRIMARY AND COMMON SCHOOLS.

By F. A. ADAMS,

AUTHOR OF MENTAL AND WRITTEN ARITHMETIC.

NEW YORK:
PUBLISHED BY D. BIXBY, 122 FULTON-STREET.
PHILADELPHIA:
THOMAS, COWPERTHWAIT AND COMPANY.
BOSTON:
B. B. MUSSEY AND COMPANY.
1849.

PREFACE.

A GENERAL idea of this work may be obtained through the following statement of its characteristic features.

It combines a variety of operations upon the small numbers first introduced; enabling the child, by holding the number in mind, and viewing it in various ways, to get a clearer idea of it than he otherwise could.

The pupil is not conducted hastily from small numbers to large ones. Special care is taken to avoid the danger of calling his attention to numbers which are beyond his mental grasp. There can be little doubt that this apparent slowness of progress will secure the best speed in the end.

Another feature is the distinct and thorough exhibition of the decimal law of numbers, as seen in the composition of numerical words. The attention given to this point, it is believed, will remove some obstacles usually found in the student's path in his more advanced studies.

To aid the pupil's power of apprehension, numbers are represented in the early part of the work by means of dots. The child has thus placed before him a natural, instead of an arbitrary sign; the sign of a number itself, instead of the sign of its name.

The subject of Fractions is treated in connection with the actual division of a line on the slate, or the blackboard. Thus the pupil not only sees the unit, and its parts, but he *makes* the unit and the parts into which it is divided. He thus receives the idea through both the eye and the hand. The drawing of figures from the directions in the book is only an extension of the discipline begun in the divisions of the line.

The use of the slate, in drawing and dividing lines, and in constructing figures, will increase the pupils' pleasure in the study; and, at the same time, will serve to cultivate the powers of the eye and the hand.

The Lessons and Tables have been constructed with a view to render the pupils *quick* in their habits of calculation. Too little attention is given in schools to this important point. The slowness of calculation unavoidable at first, often becomes the pupil's fixed habit, impeding his progress in all the higher stages of the study. Many precious hours, thus lost, might be saved by timely efforts directed to this specific point. An attempt is here made to afford to teachers some aid in securing this desirable object.

ORANGE, NEW JERSEY, *Oct.* 4, 1848.

ARITHMETIC.

PART FIRST.

THE NUMBERS GIVEN OR REQUIRED NOT EXCEEDING TEN.

LESSON FIRST.

ADDITION.

A - - - - - - - - - - - - - - ●
B - - - - - - - - - - - - - - ● ●
C - - - - - - - - - - - - - - ● ● ●
D - - - - - - - - - - - - - - ● ● ● ●

A. QUESTIONS TO BE ANSWERED BY THE PUPIL FROM THE BOOK.

What large letters do you see on this page?
Are they on the right or the left side of the page?
What is the first letter? What is the next?
What is the next? What is the last letter?

What do you see opposite to the letters, on the right side of the page?
How many dots are there opposite to the letter A?
How many dots are there opposite to B?
How many dots are there opposite to C?
How many dots are there opposite to D?

Find the line that has one dot on it: what letter is opposite to that dot?

What letter is opposite to the line of two dots?

What letter is opposite to the three dots?

What letter is opposite to the four dots?

Let the Class answer together.

How many are one and two?*
How many are one and three?
How many are one and four?
How many are two and three?
How many are two and four?
How many are four and two?
How many are three and two?

B. If you have two marbles in one hand and three in the other, how many have you in both?

If there are three roses on one bush and two on another, how many are there on both?

If there are four apples on one plate and two on another, how many are there on both?

If there are two chairs in the room and you bring in four more, how many will there be in the room then?

If you find three red apples under one tree, and two green ones under another, how many apples do you find in all?

If there are three girls sitting on one seat and four on another, how many are there on both?

If there are four windows in one end of a house, and two in the other, how many windows are there in both ends?

Let the Class answer together.

Three and one?	Three and two?	Two and three?
Four and one?	Four and two?	Four and three?
Three and four?	One and four?	Two and four?

One and two and three?†	Two and one and three?
Two and three and one?	One and three and two?
Three and one and two?	Three and two and one?

* Note A. † Note B

One and two and four?
Two and one and four?
Four and one and two?
One and three and four?
Three and one and four?
Four and one and three?
One and four and two?
Two and four and one?
Four and two and one?
One and four and three?
Three and four and one?
Four and three and one?

LESSON SECOND.

SUBTRACTION.

A. If there are five sheep in a pasture, and only three of them in sight, how many are out of sight?

If there are five apples on a plate, and Mary takes away two of them, how many will be left?

If you have five pears, and eat one and give away two, how many will you have left?

If there are six plums on a plate, and John eats one of them, how many will be left?

If Mary then eats two more, how many will be left?

If there are six windows in the side of a house, and only three of them are closed, how many are there open?

If you have six chestnuts and lose four of them, how many will you then have?

If you make seven dots on your slate, and rub out three of them, how many will there be left?

There are four boys reciting together in Arithmetic; the teacher makes eight marks on the blackboard, and then rubs out four of those marks; how many are left?

The teacher then makes four marks more, and rubs out as many as there are boys in the class; how many does he rub out?

How many marks are left?

B. Questions to be answered by the Class together without the Book.

Teacher. Now we will take some number and I will divide it into two parts, and tell you what one of the parts is, and you must all tell me what the other part is. We will first take the number *Three*. Observe, I have divided the number three, in my mind, into two parts. What do you think they are?

Class. We cannot tell.

Teacher. Well, I am not going to tell you; but I shall tell you *one* of the parts, and then you must tell me the *other*. Now, be ready; my part is *one*, what is your part?

Class. Two.

Teacher. Very well; now put the two parts together, and see what they make. One and two are how many?

Now, I will divide the number Three again, and this time my part is *two;* what is your part?

Now, I will take the number Four. Be ready, all, to give me your part as soon as I shall give you mine. I have divided it, and my part is *one;* what is yours? [*Ans.*]

Very well; now I have divided it again, and this time my part is two; what is yours?

And once more I have divided it, and this time my part is three?

Now that you understand it, we will go a little faster. We will take the number Five. Be ready, all, to give me the second part of it. *One—Two—Three—Four?*

Now take the number Six. Give me promptly the second part. *One—Two—Four—Three—Five?*

Seven.*

First Part.		*Second Part.*
Three	- - - - -	
Two	- - - - -	
Four	- - - - -	
Six	- - - - -	
Five	- - - - -	
One	- - - - -	

* Note C.

Eight.

First Part.		*Second Part.*
Two	- - - - -	
One	- - - - -	
Three	- - - - -	
Four	- - - - -	
Six	- - - - -	
Five	- - - - -	
Seven	- - - - -	

LESSON THIRD.

ADDITION AND SUBTRACTION.

A. A man has five sheep; he then buys one sheep more, and afterwards sells one: how many has he then?

If a man has five sheep, and buys one more, and then sells two, how many will he then have?

If a man has six sheep, and loses one of them, and buys two more, how many will he have then?

John has four cents; his father gives him three more, and then John spends four of them: how many cents will he have left?

William has eight cents, and Mary has five: William spends two of his; how many more than Mary will he then have?

John has four cents, and he earns four more; how many will he then have?

He then spends two for pencils, and two for a sponge; how many cents will he have left?

If you make five marks on a slate, and rub out two of them, and then make three more, how many will there be on the slate?

There are six apples on a stand: James puts on two more, and that makes three of the first ones roll off; how many are there on the stand then?

If four of the apples are then taken off the stand, how many will remain on it?

A man has seven cows: he sells two, and buys three; how many has he then?

Charles has two cents in the morning; he earns three cents in the forenoon, and two more in the afternoon, and then spends four of them: how many cents will he have left?

If Jane has eight cents, and spends three for some tape and four for a thimble, how many cents will she have left?

B. Two and three and one are how many?
One and two and one and three are how many?
Two and two and one and two are how many?
Two and one and two and two are how many?

COLUMNS TO BE ADDED.*

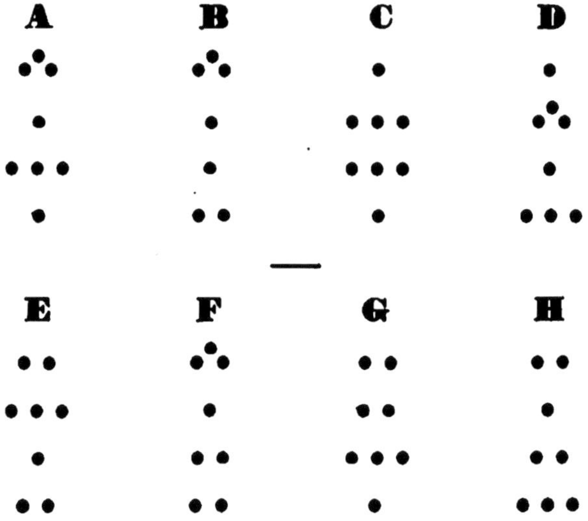

* Note D.

LESSON FOURTH.

ADDITION.

A. If you find four apples under one tree, and three under another, and two under another, how many do you find in all ?

If John eats three peaches, and James eats four, and Charles eats two, how many do they all eat ?

If there are five windows in one row, and four in another, how many are there in both ?

If you have four cherries in one hand, and six in the other, how many have you in both ?

If you make four marks in one row, and three in another, and three in another, how many do you make in all ?

If you spend five cents for a book, and four cents for some paper, how many do you spend in all ?

B. Two and three and four are how many ?
How many are two and four and three ?
Three and two and four ? Three and four and two ?
Four and three and two ? Four and two and three ?
One and two and three and four ?
One and three and two and four ?
One and two and four and three ?
One and three and four and two ?
Two and one and three and four ?
Two and one and four and three ?
Two and three and one and four ?
Two and three and four and one ?
Three and one and two and four ?
Three and four and one and two ?
Three and one and four and two ?
Four and one and three and two ?
Four and two and one and three ?
Four and three and two and one ?
Four and three and one and two ?

COLUMNS TO BE ADDED.

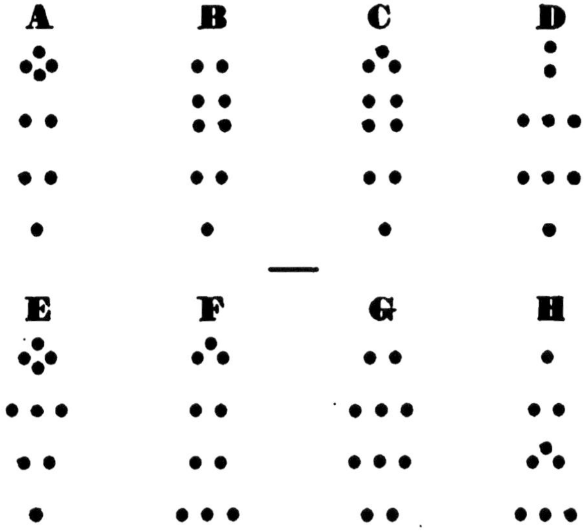

LESSON FIFTH.

ADDITION AND SUBTRACTION.

A. If you have six marbles in one hand and four in the other, how many have you in both?

If you have seven cents, and earn three more, and then spend two of them, how many will you have left?

If you have in both hands nine cents, and seven of them are in your right hand, how many are there in your left?

John gives Charles four apples, and then Charles has nine; how many had he before John gave him any?

If you have nine chestnuts, and give four of them to one person, and three to another, how many will you have left?

A man has eight dollars: he receives two more, and then pays away five dollars; how many has he left?

If there are ten cows in a pasture, and seven of them are in sight, how many are out of sight?

If you receive six cents, and spend four of them, and then receive seven cents more, how many will you then have?

Jane had nine peaches: she gave five to Mary, and the rest to Charles; did she give as many to Charles as she gave to Mary?

John makes ten marks on his slate, four of them at the top, and the rest at the bottom; how many more are there at the bottom than at the top?

B. *Let the Class give the second part of the numbers divided, as soon as the first part is given by the Teacher.**

Nine.

First Part.		*Second Part.*
Four	- - - - -	
Three	- - - - -	
Six	- - - - -	
Five	- - - - -	
Seven	- - - - -	
One	- - - - -	
Eight	- - - - -	
Two	- - - - -	

Ten.

First Part.		*Second Part.*
Three	- - - - -	
Four	- - - - -	
One	- - - - -	
Five	- - - - -	
Seven	- - - - -	
Six	- - - - -	
Two	- - - - -	
Eight	- - - - -	
Nine	- - - - -	

* Note B.

Six from ten leaves how many?

Seven from ten?	Three from ten?
Eight from ten?	One from ten?
Five from ten?	Four from ten?
Five from nine?	Seven from nine?
Four from nine?	Three from nine?
Two from nine?	One from nine?

LESSON SIXTH.

NUMBERS IN TWO EQUAL PARTS.

A. Mr. B. brought in four apples and laid them on the table for John and James, and told John, who was the oldest, that he might divide them equally: John went and took three of them, leaving James the rest; was that dividing them equally?

If Sarah has two apples to divide equally between herself and Jane, how will she divide them?

Julia has three apples to divide between herself and Mary; if she keeps one herself, and gives two to Mary, will that be dividing them equally?

If she gives one to Mary and keeps two herself, will that be dividing them equally?*

Charles has six chestnuts for himself and John, how can he divide them so that one shall have just as many as the other?

There are eight girls reciting in a class: they stand in two rows, and there are just as many in one row as in the other; how many are there in each row?

Charles brings in ten apples, and tells Mary to put them on two plates, so as to have just as many on one plate as on the other; how many will there be on each plate? (Those who have slates can make a picture of the plates on their slates, making dots for the apples.)

* Note F.

B.—*Exercise for the whole Class.*

Now, I am going to divide the number Four into two parts. Be ready, and tell me the second part. The first part is One. [*Here the Class will give the other part.*] Are the two parts alike, or not alike?

Again, I will divide Four; this time the first part is Three. [*The Class answers.*] Are the two parts now alike, or not alike?

Again, the first part is Two. ——. Are the two parts now alike, or not? [*After the Class have answered.*] Yes, the two parts are now alike, that is, they are equal to each other.

Now, we will take the number Six, and divide it. Be ready to answer. The first part is Two. ——. Are the two parts equal, or not equal?

Again I divide it; now the first part is One. ——. Are the parts equal, or not equal?*

Again, the first part is Four. ——. Are the parts equal, or not equal?

Again, the first part is Three. ——. Are the parts equal, or not equal?

The number Eight: the first part Three. ——. Are the parts equal, or not equal?

The first part Five. —— Equal, or not equal?

How then will you divide it so as to make the two parts equal?

Now can you divide the number Ten into two equal parts?

What are they?

If I hold out four plums in my hand, and ask you to take half of them, how many would you take?†

How many would be left in my hand?

In order to get one half of four, into how many parts would you divide four?

Into equal, or unequal parts?

Now tell me, what is one half of two?

What is one half of six?

What is one half of eight?

What is one half of ten?

* Note G. † Note H.

LESSON SEVENTH.

WHOLE NUMBERS OBTAINED FROM THEIR HALVES.

A. Mr. B. bought some oranges, and gave half of them to John, and the rest to James; what part of them did James have? John's half was two oranges; how many did James have for his part?

Two is one half of some number; what is the other half? What is the whole number?

Charles has some chestnuts: one half of them he gives away, and keeps the rest; what part of them does he keep? He gave away three, how many had he in all?

William has one dollar in his pocket, which is half of all the money he has; how many dollars has he?

Four is one half of some number; what is the other half? What is the whole number?

Five is one half of some number; what is the number?

Exercise for the whole Class.

Whole Number.	*One Half.*	*The other Half.*
● ●	- -	- -
● ● ● ●	- -	- -
● ● ● ● ● ●	- -	- -
● ● ● ● ● ● ● ●	- -	- -
● ● ● ● ● ● ● ● ● ●	- -	- -

One Half.	*The other Half.*	*The Whole Number*
●	- -	- -
● ●	- -	- -
● ● ●	- -	- -
● ● ● ●	- -	- -
● ● ● ● ●	- -	- -

B. Mr. C. has five marbles to give to Charles and John: if he gives Charles two and John three, will that be dividing them equally? If he gives John two and Charles three, will he divide them equally then?

Is two one half of five? What is two one half of? Is two more or less than half of five? Is three one half of five?* What is three one half of? Is three more or less than one half of five?

Can you divide the number three into halves?†
Can you divide the number four into halves?
What other number can you divide into halves?
Name some numbers that you cannot divide into halves.

All those numbers that can be divided into halves are called *even numbers*.

What is the smallest even number?
What is the next? What is the next?
Name all the even numbers from two up to ten.

LESSON EIGHTH.

UNEQUAL AND EQUAL PARTS.

A. Henry had eight cents: he earned two more, and then spent half of all he had; how many cents had he left?

James has four peaches, and Charles has just as many as James; how many have they both?

John has five apples, and Charles has three: John gives to Charles enough to make his number and Charles's equal; how many does he give to him?

Jane finds five plums under one tree, four under another, and one under another: she gives half of them all to Sarah; how many does she keep herself?

If you make three marks in one row, and four in another, and one in another, and then rub out half of them, how many will be left?

* Note J. † Note K.

John asked Henry how many nuts he had: said Henry, "I shall not tell you, but I will tell you this—I have two in my right hand, and three in my left, and adding these together makes half of the whole; and now you may find out if you can." How many had he?

Mary had ten pears: she ate one, and gave three to James, and then divided the rest equally with Henry; how many did Henry receive?

A boy had nine cents: he gave three for a pencil, and then spent half of the rest for nuts; how many cents had he left?

Sarah has four pears, Mary has as many as Sarah, and William has half as many as Sarah; if they put them all together, how many will there be?

John has five peaches; if he puts three of them away, and then gives half of the rest to James, how many will James have?

B. Mr. C. told James and William that, if they would eat no more apples that day, they should, the next morning, have all that were found under the tree. The next morning Mr. C. brought in five apples to divide between the two boys. "But," says James, "if William has three I shall have only two, and if I have three William will have only two." "Well," said Mr. C., "I will take away one and keep it for you, and see if you can divide the rest." When they had divided the rest, their father laid the apple he had taken upon the table, and said, "Now, see if you can divide that." "Oh, yes!" said William, "if I can get a knife." How many apples did each of the boys have, after they were divided?

Charles and Henry have five oranges; if each is to have half of them, how many will each one have?

How can you divide three apples into two equal parts?

Mrs. C. laid seven peaches on the table, and told Mary she should have one half of them if she would divide them equally with Jane. While Mary was thinking how to divide them, William came in and said, "You had better divide six first, and then you can think about the other." How many do you think Mary gave to Jane,—and how many did she have herself?

If you had nine oranges, could you divide the whole into two equal parts?

Which is easiest, to divide eight oranges into two equal parts, or to divide nine oranges? Why?

Which is easiest, to divide five apples into two equal parts, or to divide six apples? Why?

Which is easiest, to divide three apples, or four apples, into halves? Why?

Those numbers which you cannot divide into halves without dividing some one of them by itself, are called odd numbers.

Tell me now, is the number Three an even number, or an odd? Why?

Is the number Two even or odd? What is one half of it?

Is the number Three even or odd? What is one half of it?

Is Four even or odd? What is one half of it?

Tell me whether the numbers are even or odd, as I call them—One? Two? Three? Four? Five? Six? Seven? Eight? Nine? Ten?

What are all the even numbers between one and ten?

What are all the odd numbers between one and ten?

PART SECOND.

THE NUMBERS GIVEN OR REQUIRED NOT EXCEEDING TWENTY.

LESSON NINTH.

ADDITION.

A - - - - - - - - - * ● ● ● ● ● ● ● ● ● ●

B - - - - - - - - * * ● ● ● ● ● ● ● ● ● ●

C - - - - - - - * * * ● ● ● ● ● ● ● ● ● ●

D - - - - - - * * * * ● ● ● ● ● ● ● ● ● ●

E - - - - - * * * * * ● ● ● ● ● ● ● ● ● ●

F - - - - * * * * * * ● ● ● ● ● ● ● ● ● ●

G - - - * * * * * * * ● ● ● ● ● ● ● ● ● ●

H - - * * * * * * * * ● ● ● ● ● ● ● ● ● ●

J - * * * * * * * * * ● ● ● ● ● ● ● ● ● ●

K * * * * * * * * * * ● ● ● ● ● ● ● ● ● ●

QUESTIONS TO BE ANSWERED FROM THE BOOK.

A. How many stars are there in the line A? How many dots? Adding them together, how many?

How many stars in the line B? How many dots? How many of both?

What is there in the line C?* What number do the stars and the dots together make?

What is there in the line D? What number do they all make?

* Note L.

What is there in the line E? What number do they all make?

What is there in the line F? How many parts has the line F? What is the first part? What is the second part? Put the two parts together, what number does it make?

What is the first part of the line G? What is the second part? What number do these two parts make?

What is the first part of the line H? What is the second part? Putting them together, what number does it make?

Describe the line J, and add its parts.

Describe the line K, and add its parts.

B. *Exercise for the Class.*

Attend carefully now to the word which I am going to speak. Sixteen. What two numbers did I name then?

Again listen. Seventeen. What two numbers are there in the word?

What are the two numbers expressed by Eighteen? Nineteen? Sixteen? Fifteen? Fourteen? Thirteen?

Twelve is also made up of two old words, meaning *two* and *ten*; and *Eleven* means *one* and *ten*.

LESSON TENTH.

ADDITION AND SUBTRACTION.

A. John had five cents, and his father gave him ten more; how many had he then? Five and ten are how many? Ten and five?

William found ten apples under one tree, and seven under another, how many are ten and seven? How many are seven and ten?

If you pay six cents for a pencil, and ten for a book, how many cents do you pay for both? Six and ten are how many? Ten and six?

A man bought a pound of raisins for nine cents, and a pound of sugar for ten: how many cents did he pay for both? Ten and nine are how many?

How many are eight and ten? Ten and eight?

William had three marbles in his hand and ten in his pocket; how many had he in all?

Samuel had ten marbles: he bought four more, and lost one of them; how many had he left?

A man had seven sheep in one pasture and ten in another; how many had he in both? After selling four of them how many had he left?

A grocer bought eighteen barrels of flour; after selling ten barrels, how many barrels had he left?

There are fifteen pears on a branch: five of them are picked off; how many remain?

B. *Exercise for the Class.*

If you have the number Sixteen, and take away six, what number will be left? If you take away ten from sixteen, what will be left?

If you have eighteen, and take away eight, what will be left? If you take away ten from eighteen, what will be left?

Be ready now, and give me the two parts of each number I name, remembering that one of the parts must be ten. Fourteen? Thirteen? Seventeen? Nineteen? Fifteen? Eighteen? Sixteen? Twenty? Twelve? Eleven?

C. What are even numbers?

What is the smallest even number?

What is the next even number?

Name all the even numbers from two up to ten.

What is the next even number above ten? What is one half of it?

What is the next even number above twelve? What is one half of it?

Name all the even numbers from ten up to twenty.

The Answers to the following Questions may be found with a Slate.

What is one half of ten?
What is one half of twelve?
What is one half of fourteen?
What is one half of sixteen?
What is one half of eighteen?
What is one half of nineteen?

Charles went to a pear-tree and brought in five pears; he went out again, and brought in five more: how many times did he bring in five pears?

How many are twice five pears?

How many are twice four? Twice three? Twice two? Twice one?

If you lay down six apples on the table, and then lay down six more, how many times six would that be?

Twice six are how many?

Twice seven are how many?

Twice eight? Twice nine? Twice ten?

When a number is repeated several times, it is said to be Multiplied. The number it is multiplied by is called the Multiplier; the number which is multiplied is called the Multiplicand. Both the numbers are called Factors; and the number obtained by multiplying the factors together is called the Product.

LESSON ELEVENTH.

COLUMNS TO BE ADDED.

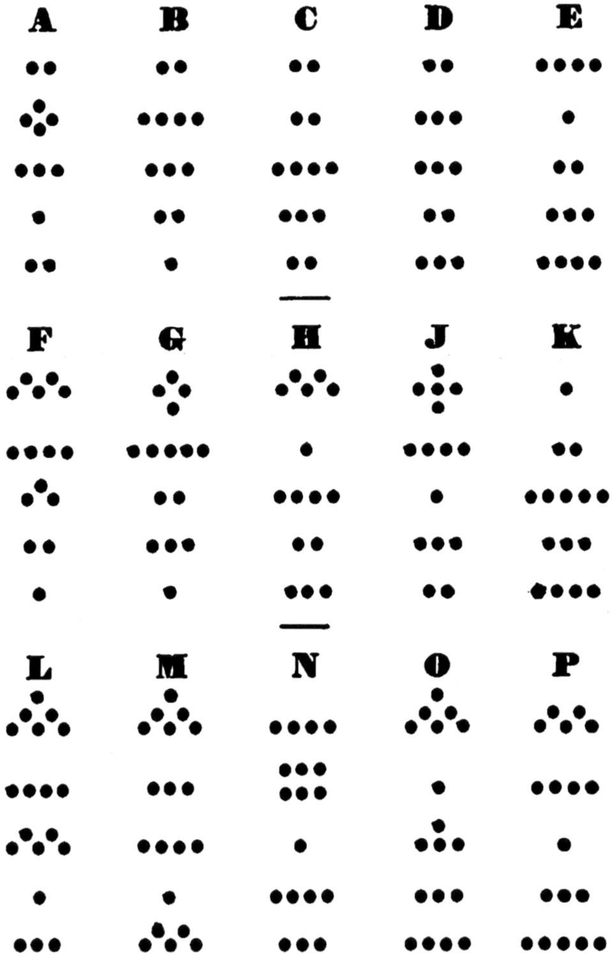

B. If you give seven cents for some peaches, and four for a melon, and five for a pineapple; how many cents do you give for them all?

If there are eight boys in one class, and five in another, and four in another, how many are there in all?

If a man spends nine dollars at one time, four at another, and three at another, how many dollars does he spend in the whole?

If a man earns seven dollars one week, six dollars the next week, and five dollars the next, how many dollars does he earn in the three weeks?

A drover bought six sheep of one man, seven of another, and five of another, and then sold eight of them; how many had he left?

Three boys are playing at marbles: the first has nine marbles, the second six, and the third five; how many marbles have they all?

A man pays nine dollars for a coat, four for a hat, three for a vest, and four for a pair of boots; how many dollars do they all cost?

Mr. A. goes out in the morning with ten dollars in his pocket, he receives from Mr. B. seven dollars, and afterwards pays to Mr. C. nine dollars; how many dollars has he left?

John finds four pears under one tree, five under another, and three under another: he gives half of the whole to William, and two of the remainder to Jane; how many had he left?

Jane has eight cents, Mary has as many as Jane, and Susan has four; how many have they all?

James has six peaches, Charles has as many as James and one over; how many have they both?

Says Thomas to Joseph, "I have eight chestnuts in my right hand, and half as many in my left; if you can tell how many I have in both hands, you shall have half of the whole:" how many would Joseph get if he told right?

A. has eight marbles, B. has half as many as A., C. has half as many as B., and D. has half as many as C.: how many have they all?

PART THIRD.

INTRODUCING NUMBERS GREATER THAN TWENTY.

LESSON TWELFTH.

A. What two parts make Fourteen, letting ten be one of the parts? In the same way what are the two parts of fifteen? Of sixteen? Of seventeen? Of eighteen? Of thirteen? Of nineteen?

Now, instead of making a row of dots for the ten, we will make one dot with a ring round it for ten; thus ⊙. Remember, whenever you see that to call it *ten*. Instead of putting it at the right hand of the stars, as we did the ten dots before, we shall now put it at the left hand.

A - - - - ⊙ ⊙ *

B - - - - ⊙ ⊙ * *

C - - - - ⊙ ⊙ * * *

D - - - - ⊙ ⊙ * * * *

E - - - - ⊙ ⊙ * * * * *

F - - - - ⊙ ⊙ * * * * * *

G - - - - ⊙ ⊙ * * * * * * *

H - - - - ⊙ ⊙ * * * * * * * *

J - - - - ⊙ ⊙ * * * * * * * * *

K - - - - ⊙ ⊙ ⊙

QUESTIONS TO BE ANSWERED FROM THE BOOK.

How many tens are there in the line A? Two tens is equal to what number? Is there any thing besides the two tens? Two tens and one make what number?

What is there in the line B, and what number does it make?

What is there in the line C, and what number does it make?

What is there in the line D, and what number does it make?

What is there in the line E, and what number does it make?

What is the number expressed in the line F? In the line G? In the line H? In the line J? In the line K?

B. How will you express on your slates, in the same way as is done in the table of this lesson, the number Ten? Twenty? Thirty?

How will you express Thirty-one? Thirty-two? Thirty-three? Thirty-four? Thirty-five?

How many tens are there in forty?

How would you express forty on the slate, by the signs used in this lesson? Forty-one? Five tens, or Fifty? Fifty-two?

LESSON THIRTEENTH.

ADDITION AND SUBTRACTION.

A. A man had twenty sheep: he bought five more, and then sold three of them; how many had he left?

A man had twenty-two dollars, and paid away three of them; how many had he left?

A market-woman had twenty apples: she bought eight more, and after selling six of them, she counted what she had left; how many had she?

Twenty and five and four and one are how many?

Twenty and six and three and three are how many?

How many are twenty-seven and five? Twenty-seven and six? Twenty-seven and seven?

If you had twenty apples, and lost one, and found two more, how many would you then have?

There are thirty apples in a basket; if three should be taken out, how many would remain? If four more should then be put in, how many would there be?

If you have thirty-six cents, and spend seven of them, how many will you have left?

A boy has twenty marbles: he plays three games; in the first he loses four, in the second he gains six, and in the third he loses five; how many has he when he leaves off playing?

Mr. B. is twenty-eight years old when his son is born; how old is Mr. B. when his son is seven years old?

How many are twenty and five and three and eight?

COLUMNS TO BE ADDED.

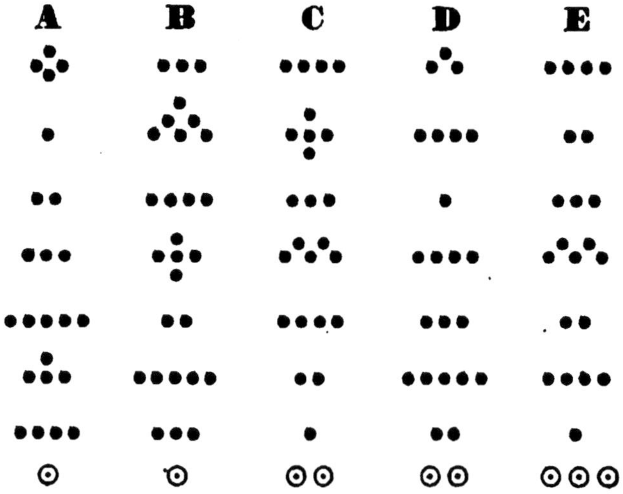

LESSON FOURTEENTH.

DIVISION INTO THREE EQUAL PARTS.

A. Jane had six peaches to divide between herself and Sarah and Henry; how must she divide them so that one may have just as many as another?

Can you make six dots on your slate, making a part of them in one place, a part in another, and a part in another, and have the parts equal to each other? How many parts would there be? How many dots would there be in each part?

If there are six oranges on three plates, and just as many on one plate as on another, how many are there on each?

Into how many parts do you divide the six oranges? Are the parts all equal? If you had divided the oranges into two equal parts, what would one of the parts be called?

If you divide a number or thing into three equal parts, one of the parts is *one third* of the whole.

What is one third of three?

What is one third of six?

If you had nine pears to put in three plates, so that each plate should have the same number, how many would you put in each plate? How many would there be on two plates?

What is one third of nine? What is two thirds of nine?

A	• • •	• •	• • • •
B	• • •	• • •	• • •
C	• • • •	• • •	• • • • •
D	• • •	• • • • • •	• • •

B. How many dots are there in the line A? Into how many parts are they divided? Are the parts all equal? Is the number then divided into thirds?

How many dots in the line B? Is the number divided into thirds? Why?

How many dots are there in the line C? Is the number divided into thirds? Why?

Is the number twelve in the line D divided into thirds?

Make a line of twelve dots on your slate, and divide it into thirds.

What is one third of twelve? What is two thirds of twelve?

Make a straight line on your slate, and divide it into three equal parts.

What is one of the parts called? What are two of the parts called? Three of the parts?

How many thirds of the line are there in the whole line?

What is one half of twelve? What is one third of twelve?

Which is greater—one half of twelve, or one third of twelve?

Draw on your slate two straight lines of equal length: divide the upper line into halves, and the lower line into thirds; which is greater—one half, or one third?

LESSON FIFTEENTH.

DIVISION.

A. Mrs. D. has four apples which she wishes to divide equally among John, Henry, and Susan; how must she divide them?

What is one third of three? What is one third of four?

If you had four oranges to divide into three equal parts, what would one of the parts be?

If a man distributes four bushels of corn equally among three persons, how much would each receive?

Draw on your slate four equal lines; how will you find one third of the whole?

What is one third of four dollars?

If you had divided four apples equally among three boys, and then should divide another equally among them, how many apples and how many thirds would each of them have?

How would you divide five oranges equally among three boys?

How would you divide six oranges equally among three boys?

What is one third of six? What is one third of three? Of four? Of five?

John, James, and Charles have two melons to be divided equally among them;—says Charles, "Let us divide one first:" what part of a melon would each one have after they were both divided?

Draw two equal lines on your slate, and find one third of them.

One third of two is what part of one?

What is one third of six?

What is one third of seven?

What is one third of eight?

What is one third of nine?

What is one third of ten?

What is one third of eleven?

What is one third of twelve?

B. James finds four apples under one tree, and two under another: he gives half of them to Charles; how many does he keep himself?

William has eight cents: he loses two of them and then spends one third of the remainder; how many does he spend? How many has he left?

James has seven oranges, and Samuel has two: they put them all together, and then divide them into three equal parts; how many are there in each part?

If you have seven chestnuts and lose one of them, what will one third of the remainder be?

Mr. A. has six oranges: he lays half of them on one plate for Sarah, and one third of them on another plate for John, and keeps the rest himself; how many will he have himself?

Henry and Charles have each six cents: Henry spends half of his, and Charles spends one third of his; how much more does Henry spend than Charles?

John has nine cents, and Samuel has eight: Samuel spends half of his, and John one third of his; how many cents has each of them left?

There are twelve apples in a basket: if half of them are red, and a third of them green, and the rest yellow; how many yellow ones are there?

Which is the most—one third of twelve, or one half of ten?

Henry says he can put his marbles in three rows, with two marbles in one row, three in the next, and four in the next: "Now," says he to George, "if you will tell what two thirds of them all are, you may have the other third;" how many marbles would George get if he told right?

C. *Add each Column, and find half of its sum.*

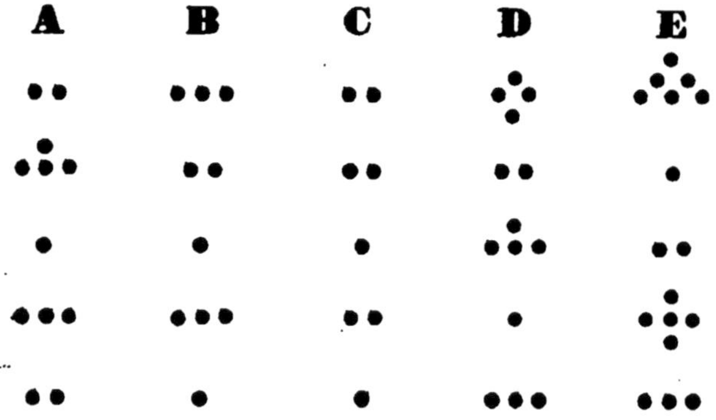

Add each Column, and find one third of its sum.

F G H J K

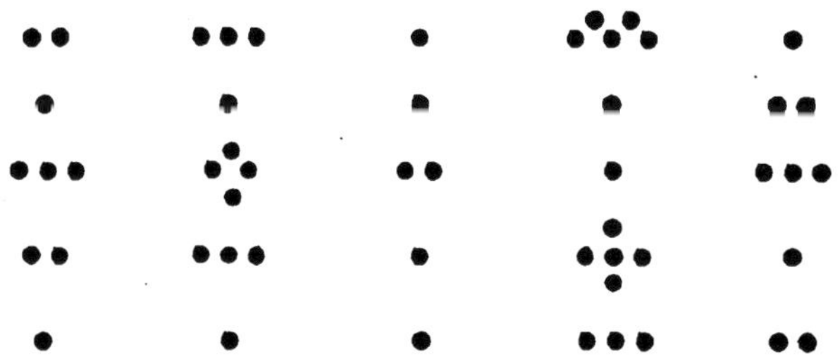

LESSON SIXTEENTH.

DIVISION INTO FOUR EQUAL PARTS.

A. There are eight boys in school: they are sitting on four seats, with the same number on each seat; how many are there on each seat?

When a number or thing is divided into four equal parts, one of those parts is a fourth of the whole.

What is one fourth of eight?

If you divide twelve into two equal parts, what part of twelve will each of the parts be? How many will each part be?

If you then divide each of those parts into two equal parts, into how many equal parts will the twelve be divided?

When any thing or number is divided into four equal parts, what is one of the parts called?

What is one fourth of twelve?

How would you get one fourth part of an apple?

If you should divide four apples into four equal parts, what part of the four apples would each of the parts be? How many apples would each part be?

If you had five apples to divide into four equal parts, what would you do first? What would you do next?

What is one fourth of five apples?

What is one fourth of five dollars?

What is one fourth of two apples?

First find one half of two. Draw a line on your slate, and divide it into halves; then divide it into fourths.

One half is how many fourths?

Two halves are how many fourths?

If you had six apples, how could you divide them into four equal parts?

How could you divide three apples into four equal parts?

A man had seven bushels of wheat, which he wished to divide into four equal parts, how much would there be in each part?

If you had eight oranges to give to four persons, how would you divide them so that the parts should all be equal?

If you had nine oranges to divide into four equal parts, how many could you divide into fourths without cutting an orange? What would you then do with what was left? What would one fourth of the whole be?

What would be one fourth of ten oranges?

B. *Add each Column, and find one half of its sum, and then one fourth of its sum.*

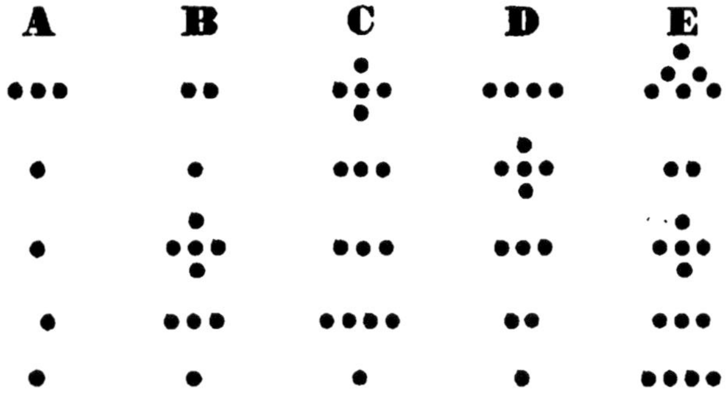

LESSON SEVENTEENTH.

MULTIPLICATION.

A. Henry is told to go into the garden and bring in some melons: he goes three times, and each time brings in two melons; how many does that make? If he had gone four times, bringing two at each time, how many would he have brought?

How many are three times two? Twice two? Four times two? Five times two?

Make two dots on your slate six times.

How many are six times two?
How many are seven times two?
How many are eight times two?
How many are nine times two?
How many are ten times two?

B. A man eats three meals a day; how many meals does he eat in two days? How many meals does he eat in three days? How many in four days? In six days? In seven days?

A man travels three miles an hour; how many miles will he travel in two hours? How many miles will he travel in three hours? In four hours? In five hours?

A man pays three dollars a week for his board; how much will he pay for his board for two weeks? How much for three weeks? How much for six weeks? For seven weeks?

C. TABLE FOR MULTIPLICATION.

	A	B	C	D	E
Ten times	••	•••	••••	•••••	••••••
Nine times	••	•••	••••	•••••	••••••
Eight times	••	•••	••••	•••••	••••••
Seven times	••	•••	••••	•••••	••••••
Six times	••	•••	••••	•••••	••••••
Five times	••	•••	••••	•••••	••••••
Four times	••	•••	••••	•••••	••••••
Three times	••	•••	••••	•••••	••••••
Twice	••	•••	••••	•••••	••••••
Once	••	•••	••••	•••••	••••••

First Mode of Recitation.—Begin with the column A, "Once two is two; twice two are four; three times," &c. Then take the column B in the same way; then the column C, and so on.

Second Mode of Recitation.—Begin at the bottom, at the number two, and proceed across the page, thus: "Once two is two; once three is three," &c. Next multiply by two: "Twice two are four; twice three are six; twice four are eight," &c. Then multiply by three; then by four, and so on.

Third Mode of Recitation.—Give the products only, without stating the process, first taking each column by itself. Thus column A would give the products—two, four, six, eight, &c. The column B—three, six, nine, &c. Next, take the table in horizontal lines, multiplying each number in the line as required by the words at the left hand of it. Thus the line marked "Five times" would give ten, fifteen, twenty, &c.

LESSON EIGHTEENTH.

RELATION OF UNITS AND THIRDS.

A. If you divide three oranges into three equal parts, how many oranges will one of the parts be?

What part of the whole will each orange be?

How many thirds will make up the whole?

One apple is what part of three apples?

Two is what part of three?

Six is how many times three?

Seven is how many times three? *Ans.* Six is twice three, and one is one third of three; twice three and one third of three.

Eight is how many times three?

Nine is how many times three?

Ten is how many times three?

Eleven is how many times three?

Twelve is how many times three?

Thirteen is how many times three?

Fourteen is how many times three?

Fifteen is how many times three?

B. Draw four equal, straight lines on your slate; divide each line into three equal parts.

How many thirds of a line are there in one line?

How many thirds of a line are there in two lines?

How many thirds in three lines? In four lines?

How many thirds of an apple are there in three apples?

How many thirds of a dollar are there in four dollars?

Mr. G. divides three melons among several boys, giving one third of a melon to each person; how many boys were there?

Mr. A. divides four bushels of wheat among some poor persons, giving one third of a bushel to each; how many persons did he give it to?

How many thirds are there in five whole ones?

How many thirds are there in six whole ones?

How many thirds are there in seven whole ones?

C. Draw four equal straight lines. Divide each line into three equal parts.

Count five thirds of a line; how many whole lines is it equal to?

How many whole lines is four thirds of a line equal to?

How many whole lines is six thirds equal to? Seven thirds? Eight thirds? Nine thirds? Ten thirds? Eleven thirds? Twelve thirds?

A man distributed some flour to seven persons, giving to each one third of a barrels; how many barrel did he distribute?

James gathers eight baskets of apples, each basket containing one third of a bushel; how many bushels did he gather?

William has a basket containing one third of a peck: he fills it ten times with plums; how many pecks of plums did it make?

There is a bowl containing one third of a quart: if you fill it eleven times with water, how many quarts will that be?

Twelve thirds of a hundred weight are how many hundred weight?

James finds thirteen sticks, each stick one third of a foot long; if put together, end to end, in one line, how long would it be?

LESSON NINETEENTH.

RELATION OF UNITS AND FOURTHS.

A. Draw on your slate five equal straight lines. Divide each line into four equal parts.

What is one of the parts called? What are two of the parts called? Three of the parts? How many fourths of a line are there in a whole line?

How many fourths of a line are there in two whole lines? How many fourths in three whole lines? In four whole lines? In five whole lines?

If a family consume one fourth of a bushel of potatoes a day, how long will they be in consuming two bushels? How long in consuming four bushels? How long in consuming five bushels?

If you have a dish that holds one fourth of a quart, how many times must you fill it in order to measure one quart? How many times must you fill it to measure three quarts? How many times to measure four quarts?

Count off, in the line you have drawn, seven fourths; how many whole lines is it equal to?

How many whole lines is nine fourths of a line equal to?

Eight fourths is equal to how many wholes?

Ten fourths is how many wholes? Eleven fourths?

Twelve fourths is how many wholes? Thirteen fourths?

Five quarters of a dollar is how many dollars?

Nine quarters of a dollar is how many dollars?

Ten quarters is how many dollars?

Jane was quartering some apples, when Henry came and asked her how many she had done. "There are the quarters," said she, "and you may see if you can find out." So he counted, and found twenty quarters; how many apples had Jane quartered?

B. COLUMNS TO BE ADDED, AND THEIR SUM DIVIDED.*

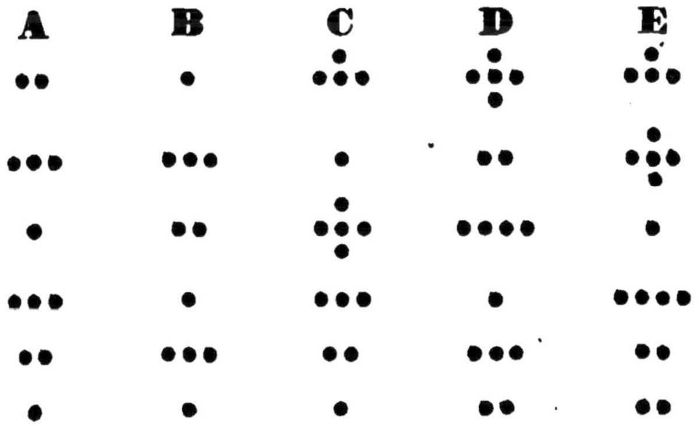

* Note M

First, Add each column, and find one half of its sum.
Second, Add each column, and find one third of its sum.
Third, Add each column, and find one fourth of its sum.

LESSON TWENTIETH.

YARDS AND FEET.

A. In one yard there are three feet; how many feet are in two yards? In three yards? In four yards?*

A man had a pole three yards long; if he cut off one yard, how many feet would there be in the remainder?

One stick is two yards long, and another is three yards long; if they are put together, end to end, how many feet long will they both be?

A room is four yards wide, and five yards long; how many feet is it in length? How many feet is it in width?

There is a stick two yards long, and another twice as long; how many feet in length is the longer stick?

There is a stick four feet long; how many feet more than a yard is it in length?

What part of a yard is one foot? Two feet?

If you have a stick five feet in length, and cut off one yard from it, what part of a yard in length will the remainder be?

John has a straight stick eleven feet long; how many yard-sticks can he make of it, and how much will he have remaining?

If three feet make one yard, how many feet are there in half a yard?

How many feet are there in a yard and a half? In two yards and a half?

James had a stick five feet long; he cut off half a yard; how many feet in length was the remainder?

There are two sticks; one is two feet in length, the other is half a yard in length: if they are put together how many feet in length will they both be? How many yards?

* Note N.

There is a room fourteen feet wide: its length is a yard and a half greater than its width; how many feet is it in length? How many yards in length?

B. If you divide a line one foot long into four equal parts, one of the parts will be just as long as the line you see below.

A

What part of a foot in length is the line A?

Draw a line on your slate twice as long as the line A; what part of a foot will the line on your slate be?

If you should draw a line three times as long as the line A, what part of a foot would it be?

If you should divide a foot into six equal parts, what part of a foot would one of the parts be?*

If you should divide a foot into eight equal parts, what part of a foot would one of the parts be?

If you divide a foot into eight equal parts, how many of those parts would there be in half of a foot? How many in one fourth of a foot?

If you should divide a foot into twelve equal parts, what part of a foot would one of the parts be? How many of the parts would there be in one half of a foot? How many of the parts would there be in one fourth of a foot? How many in three fourths of a foot?

For the purposes of measuring, a foot is divided into twelve equal parts, called inches.

How many inches are there in one foot?
How many inches are there in half of a foot?
How many inches are there in a fourth of a foot?

Draw on your slate a line one fourth of a foot long. Divide the line into inches.

Draw a line half of a foot long. Divide it into inches.

* Note O.

C. How many inches are there in one foot and a quarter?

How many inches are there in one foot and a half? In one foot and three fourths?

John has a ruler seven inches long, and James has one six inches long; what is the length of them both? If you add to their length another ruler six inches long, would they all be more, or less than a foot and a half?

How many feet are there in one yard?

How many inches are there in half a yard?

How many inches are there in a quarter of a yard?

Henry has a round ruler, and a square one: the round one is half a yard long, the square one is a foot and a quarter long; which is the longer of the two, and how much?

James has a stick a yard and a half in length: he cuts off two inches from one end, and a quarter of a foot from the other; how long is the stick then?

If you have a stick twelve inches in length, and cut off, first one third of a foot, and then one fourth of a foot, how many inches will remain?

If you draw a line two thirds of a foot in length, how many inches must you add to it to make it twelve inches in length?

LESSON TWENTY-FIRST.

MULTIPLICATION: ORDER OF FACTORS VARIED.

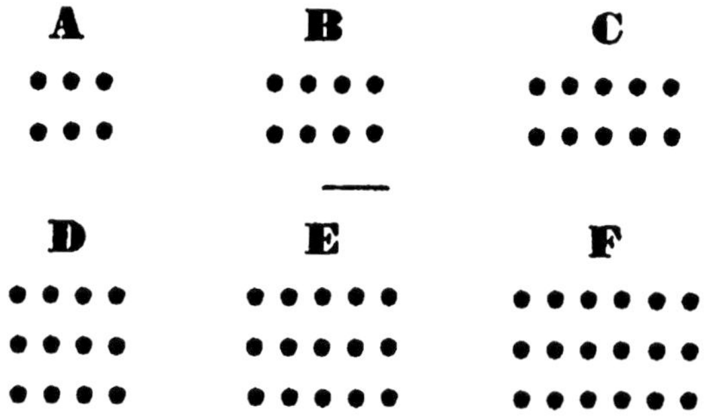

A. If you read the dots at A in horizontal lines, that is, from left to right, or from right to left, how many rows are there? How many dots in each row?

If you read the dots at A in perpendicular rows, that is, up and down, how many rows are there? How many dots in each row? How many times two dots are there at A? How many times three dots?

Twice three are how many? Three times two are how many?

How many horizontal rows are there at B? How many in each row? How many perpendicular rows? How many in each row?

Twice four are how many? Four times two?

Twice five are how many? Five times two?

At what letter can you find four times three dots? Where do you find three times four dots?

How many are three times four? Four times three?

At what letter do you find three times five dots? Five times three dots?

How many are three times five? Five times three?

How many are three times six? Six times three?

Where do you find six times three? Three times six?

How many are four times five? Five times four?

How many are four times six? Six times four?

What number must I take five times in order to make ten? Twice what number is ten?

Twelve is three times what number? Twelve is four times what number? Twelve is six times what number? Twelve is twice what number?

Sixteen is twice what number? Sixteen is eight times what number? Sixteen is four times what number?

Eighteen is twice what number? Eighteen is six times what number? Eighteen is three times what number? Eighteen is nine times what number?

B. Table for Multiplication.

	A	B	C	D
Ten times	∶∶∶•	∶∶∶∶	∶∶∶∶•	⊙
Nine times	∶∶∶•	∶∶∶∶	∶∶∶∶•	⊙
Eight times	∶∶∶•	∶∶∶∶	∶∶∶∶•	⊙
Seven times	∶∶∶•	∶∶∶∶	∶∶∶∶•	⊙
Six times	∶∶∶•	∶∶∶∶	∶∶∶∶•	⊙
Five times	∶∶∶•	∶∶∶∶	∶∶∶∶•	⊙
Four times	∶∶∶•	∶∶∶∶	∶∶∶∶•	⊙
Three times	∶∶∶•	∶∶∶∶	∶∶∶∶•	⊙
Twice	∶∶∶•	∶∶∶∶	∶∶∶∶•	⊙
Once	∶∶∶•	∶∶∶∶	∶∶∶∶•	⊙

First Mode of Recitation.—Begin with the column of sevens, at the bottom: "Once seven, twice seven, three times seven," &c. Then take the column of eights in the same way; then the column of nines; then the tens.

Second Mode.—Begin with the lowest line at the number seven: "Once seven, once eight," &c. Next take the line above: "Twice seven, twice eight," &c.

C. In a boys' school there are six seats, and five boys on each seat; in a girls' school there are seven seats, and four girls on each seat: which school has the most scholars?

James went six times to a pile of apples, and brought away eight apples each time; Henry went seven times, and brought away seven each time: which boy brought away the most?

Mr. A. rode eight hours, riding five miles each hour; Mr. B. rode seven hours, riding six miles each hour: which travelled farthest?

There is a pear orchard with nine rows of trees, and eight trees in each row; there is an apple orchard with ten rows, and seven trees in each row: which orchard has the most trees?

Mr. C. works ten days, earning eight shillings a day; Mr. D. works nine days, earning nine shillings a day: which earns the most?

D. COLUMNS OF TENS TO BE ADDED.

A	B	C	D	E
⊙	⊙ ⊙	⊙	⊙	⊙ ⊙ ⊙
⊙ ⊙	⊙	⊙ ⊙	⊙ ⊙	⊙
⊙	⊙ ⊙ ⊙	⊙ ⊙	⊙ ⊙ ⊙	⊙ ⊙
⊙	⊙	⊙	⊙	⊙ ⊙ ⊙ ⊙
⊙ ⊙	⊙ ⊙	⊙ ⊙	⊙ ⊙ ⊙	⊙ ⊙ ⊙
⊙	⊙	⊙ ⊙ ⊙	⊙	⊙ ⊙
⊙	⊙ ⊙	⊙	⊙ ⊙ ⊙	⊙

LESSON TWENTY-SECOND.

MULTIPLICATION AND DIVISION COMBINED.

A. A man worked four days, earning six shillings a day: he paid away one third of his wages for grain; how many shillings had he left?

A man works four days, earning seven shillings a day: after spending ten shillings, he gives away half of the remainder; how many shillings has he left?

James earns eight cents a day for four days: he spends twelve cents for a book, and then gives away one fourth of the remainder; how many cents has he left?

A boy buys a peck of apples for fifteen cents: he sells a part of them for six cents, and then sells the remainder for two thirds of what he gave for the whole; did he gain or lose, and how much?

William earns five cents an hour for five hours: after receiving his pay, he spends ten cents of it for a book, and one third of the remainder for some nuts; how many cents had he left?

John had twelve cents: he paid away half of a third of it for a pencil, and bought some paper, giving twice as much for the paper as he gave for the pencil; how many cents had he left?

One half of twelve is how many thirds of nine?

One half of sixteen is how many thirds of twelve?

One half of eight is how many thirds of six?

Three times two is how many fourths of twelve?

Four times three is how many halves of eight?

B. Charles has twelve pears: he gives one fourth of them to John, one fourth to James, and one third to Henry; how many has he left?

James has twelve peaches: after giving one third of them away, he eats one fourth of the remainder; how many had he then left?

What is one half of one third of twelve? First find one third of twelve.

What is one third of one half of twelve?

What is one half of two thirds of twelve? First find two thirds of twelve.

What is two thirds of one half of twelve?

What is one fourth of two thirds of twelve?

What is two thirds of one fourth of twelve?

One half of a third of twelve is what part of twelve? First find how many it is, and then find what part of twelve it is.

One third of one fourth of twelve is what part of twelve?

Two thirds of one half of twelve is what part of twelve?

C. Draw a line, and divide it into two equal parts; then divide each half into three equal parts.

One third of one half of the line is what part of the whole?

Two thirds of one half is what part of the whole?

One half of one third is what part of the whole? First find one third of the whole line.

One half of two thirds is what part of the whole?

Draw a line, and divide it into twelve equal parts.

What is one of the parts called? Two of the parts?

One half of the line is how many twelfths?

Three twelfths of the line is how many fourths?

One third of the line is how many twelfths?

Two thirds is how many twelfths?

Three fourths is how many twelfths?

One sixth is how many twelfths?

Five sixths is how many twelfths?

LESSON TWENTY-THIRD.

THE HALF AND FOURTH COMBINED—THE PECK AND GALLON.

A. In one bushel there are four pecks: how many pecks are there in two bushels? In three bushels? In four bushels?

What part of a bushel is one peck?

What part of a bushel is two pecks? Three pecks?

How many pecks are there in one bushel and a half?

How many pecks are there in two bushels and a half? In three bushels?

In one peck there are two gallons: how many gallons are there in three pecks?

How many gallons in one bushel?

How many gallons in half a bushel?

One gallon is what part of a bushel?

Two gallons is how many eighths of a bushel? How many fourths of a bushel?

Four gallons is how many eighths of a bushel?
Four gallons is how many fourths of a bushel?
Four gallons is how many halves of a bushel?

Draw a line, and divide it into eight equal parts.
How many eighths are equal to one half of the line?
How many eighths are equal to one fourth of the line?
How many eighths are equal to three fourths of the line?

B. In one gallon there are four quarts; in one quart there are two pints: how many pints are there in a gallon?
How many pints in two gallons?
What part of a gallon is one pint? Two pints?

Seven men have a gallon of beer, and drink each one pint of it; what part of a gallon did they drink? What part of a gallon remains?

A man bought two gallons of molasses; after using five quarts, how many quarts were there left?

If three pints be taken from one gallon of milk, how many pints will remain?

A man having two gallons of milk, sold half of it to A., then half of the remainder to B., and gave away half of what was then left to C.; how much did C. receive?

If from a vessel containing one gallon and a half, five pints be taken, how many pints will be left?

Draw a line, and divide it first into two equal parts; then, into four equal parts; then, into eight equal parts.
One half of the line is how many fourths?
One half of the line is how many eighths?
One fourth is how many eighths?
Three fourths is how many eighths?

PART FOURTH.

ARABIC NOTATION—FRACTIONS—DENOMINATE NUMBERS.

LESSON TWENTY-FOURTH.

ARABIC NOTATION.

A. We shall now show a different mode of expressing numbers.

For One, or	●	we write 1	
For Two,	● ●	2	
For Three,	● ● ●	3	
For Four,	● ● ● ●	4	
For Five,	● ● ● ● ●	5	
For Six,	● ● ● ● ● ●	6	
For Seven,	● ● ● ● ● ● ●	7	
For Eight,	● ● ● ● ● ● ● ●	8	
For Nine,	● ● ● ● ● ● ● ● ●	9	
For Ten,		10	meaning ten and nothing more; 0 signifying nothing.
For Eleven,		11	ten and one.
For Twelve,		12	ten and two.
For Thirteen,		13	ten and three.
For Fourteen,		14	ten and four

Can you now write on your slate the figures for Fifteen, or ten and five?

Sixteen, or ten and six? Seventeen? Eighteen? Nineteen?

Twenty is two tens and nothing more, thus 20
Twenty-one - - - - - - 21
Twenty-two - - - - - - 22

Write on the slate the figures for Twenty-three. Twenty-four. Twenty-five. Twenty-six. Twenty-seven. Twenty-eight. Twenty-nine.

Remember, the right-hand column is for all numbers up to ten, and all over ten till you come to another ten, and so on. These are called units, and the right-hand column is called the unit column. The left-hand column is for the tens.

Write the figures for three tens, or thirty. For four tens, or forty. For fifty. For sixty. For seventy. For eighty.

Write the figures for thirty-one. For forty-five. For twenty-seven. For sixty-four.

Read the Numbers in the following Columns.

A	B	C
21	61	63
33	44	71
46	38	86
85	97	91
93	82	36
85	75	59
74	41	88
66	54	23

B. *Write the following Columns on the Slate, add them, and set down their Sum.*

A	B	C	D
5	5	6	4
6	5	7	3
3	8	9	7
4	2	6	4
7	7	3	9
9	3	4	6
1	4	8	3

Add the following Columns in the Book, without setting down their Sum.

E	F	G	H
90	30	80	40
30	20	20	50
40	80	90	70
50	60	70	90
60	70	60	60
70	40	40	30
80	30	50	40
10	50	80	70
40	90	60	80

Be careful to give every number its true value, and not add the column of tens as if they were units. In column E therefore say, "Forty and ten are fifty, and eighty are a hundred and thirty," &c.

C. If the number is as great as one hundred, or ten tens, we set down the number of hundreds at the left hand of the tens.

Thus, one hundred and fifteen is written - 115
Two hundred and forty-three is written - - 243

Write three hundred and fifty-six. One hundred and sixty. Four hundred and thirty-three.

Read the Numbers expressed by the following Figures

A	B	C	D	E	F
241	317	644	634	700	504

Under A what does the figure 2 express? What does the figure 4 express? The figure 1?

Under B what does the 3 express? What does the 1 express? What does the 7 express?

Name the figures under C, and tell what each expresses. Do the same at D. At E. At F.

A man carried five loads of apples to market: the first load contained 24 bushels; the second, 17 bushels; the third, 34 bushels; the fourth, 42 bushels; the fifth, 35 bushels: how many bushels were there in all? [*To be performed without ciphering.*]

First Mode.—Add first the tens together, then add the units, and unite them into one sum. Thus, "20 bushels and 10 bushels are 30 bushels," &c.

Second Mode.—Add first the units, and after that the tens.

D. A man travelled on Monday 31 miles; on Tuesday 43 miles; on Wednesday 35 miles; on Thursday 47 miles; on Friday 36 miles; on Saturday 44 miles: how many miles did he travel in the six days?

First Mode.—Add first the tens, then the units.

Second Mode.—Begin with the units.

*Add the following Columns in the two Modes stated above.**

A	B	C	D	E
36	42	24	34	17
41	61	33	41	21
54	34	50	62	38
27	83	13	70	14
10	41	46	32	62
40	37	18	19	17

* Note P.

LESSON TWENTY-FIFTH.

PRACTICAL QUESTIONS IN FIGURES.

A. 1. James spent 10 cents on Monday, twice as much on Tuesday, and then he had 12 cents left; how many cents had he at first?

2. A man sold 3 sheep, the first for 16 shillings, the second for half as much, and the third for 12 shillings; for how many shillings did he sell them all?

3. There are 20 boys in a school, and twice as many girls: one half of the whole study grammar; how many study grammar?

4. A man travels 30 miles on Monday, and two thirds as far on Tuesday; how far does he travel on both days?

5. John has 8 marbles, James has half as many as John, and Peter has 2 more than James; how many have they all?

6. A boy going to a store paid 10 cents for some paper, 15 cents for a slate, and as much for a Geography as for both the paper and the slate; how much did he pay for them all?

7. William went 3 times to the field, bringing in 8 melons each time; he received one fourth of the whole for his pay: after giving away two, how many had he left?

8. A man journeying from home travels 24 miles the first day, 20 miles the second, 32 miles the third, and 40 miles the fourth; how far was he then from home?

9. A man works 6 days, and receives 7 shillings a day: out of this he pays 12 shillings for his board, and spends half of the remainder for provisions; how much had he then left?

10. A man sells a wagon for 30 dollars, and a harness for 10 dollars, and receives his pay in flour at 5 dollars a barrel; how many barrels did he receive?

B. 1. What number must you add to 3 to make up 10? What number must you add to 4 to make up 10? To 5? To 1? To 7? To 9? To 8?

2. If you add 10 to 10 what number do you obtain? What is the next ten to 20? What is the next ten to 40? To 60? To 50? To 70?

3. What number must you add to 24 to make up the next ten above it, that is, 30? What number must you add to 46 to make up the next ten? What number to 57? To 71? To 82? To 79?

The number thus added is called the complement.

COLUMNS OF NUMBERS FOR EXERCISES, AS DIRECTED BELOW.

A	B	C	D	E
5	15	7	22	41
7	13	9	81	78
9	21	6	34	65
3	16	4	72	43
4	18	5	64	18
6	26	8	54	15
8	17	3	97	17
1	19	6	62	19
4	28	5	32	16
3	13	1	19	14

Exercise First.—Begin at the bottom of a column and read, not the numbers, but the complement of the numbers. Thus, in column A the complements of the numbers, beginning at the bottom, are seven, six, nine, &c. In column B seven, two, one, three, &c.

Let this exercise be practised till the class can read the required numbers rapidly, without aid from the teacher.

Exercise Second.—Add the columns, beginning with the units in every instance, and naming only the sums successively made, and not the numbers added.

C. Columns for Multiplication.

Ten times	-	-	11	-	12
Nine times	-	-	11	-	12
Eight times	-	-	11	-	12
Seven times	-	-	11	-	12
Six times	-	-	11	-	12
Five times	-	-	11	-	12
Four times	-	-	11	-	12
Three times	-	-	11	-	12
Twice	-	-	11	-	12
Once	-	-	11	-	12

In learning this exercise, the numbers may first be taken separately; thus, for times 12, say "Three times ten," then "Three times 2." After sufficient practice in this way, the two numbers may be taken together.

LESSON TWENTY-SIXTH.

MULTIPLICATION.

A. 1. A man works 10 months, for 12 dollars a month; how much did his wages amount to?

2. A man buys 11 sheep for 3 dollars a head; how much did they come to?

3. What is the value of 9 barrels of flour, at 6 dollars a barrel?

4. How many cents does a boy spend in 6 days, if he spends 12 cents a day?

5. There are 7 days in a week; how many days are there in 12 weeks?

6. There are 6 working days in a week; if a man works 9 hours each day, how many hours does he work in a week?

7. Six times 4 are how many times 12? How many times 8? How many times 6? How many times 3? How many times 2?

8. Four times 12 are how many times 6? How many times 8? How many times 4? How many times 2? How many times 3?

9. Five times 12 are how many times 10? How many times 6? How many times 5? How many times 30? How many times 15? How many times 2? How many times 20?

10. Six times 6 are how many times 3? How many times 4? How many times 9? How many times 12?

B. 1. The number 4 is already divided into four equal parts—thus, ● ● ● ●; what part of the whole is one of those parts? Two of the parts? Three of the parts? Four of the parts?

2. If you divide the number 4 into two equal parts, what will one of the parts be called? One half of 4 is how many fourths of 4?

3. Draw a line, and divide it into 4 equal parts; how many fourths are equal to one half of the line? How many fourths of a dollar make half a dollar? How many fourths of a dollar make two halves of a dollar? How many fourths make three halves?

4. The number 6 is already divided into 6 equal parts; what is one of the parts called? Two of the parts? Four of the parts?

If now you divide the number into two equal parts, how many sixths is one half of the line equal to?

5. Divide the number 6 into 3 equal parts; what is one of the parts called? How many sixths does it contain? How many sixths are there in two thirds? How many sixths in three thirds?

6. Draw a line and divide it into 6 equal parts; how many of the parts make one third of the line? How many sixths make two thirds of the line?

7. The number 8 is already divided into eight equal parts; what part of the whole is one of those parts? Two of the parts? How many eighths is equal to one half? How many eighths is equal to one fourth? How many eighths are equal to two fourths? To three fourths? To four fourths?

8. Draw a line, and divide it into eighths? How many eighths make one half? One fourth? Two fourths? Three fourths?

9. One half of 12 is how many twelfths of 12? One half of 12 is how many fourths of 12?

10. One third of twelve is how many sixths of 12? One third of 12 is how many twelfths of 12?

11. One fourth of 12 is how many twelfths of 12? Three fourths of 12 are how many twelfths of 12?

12. Draw a line and divide it into halves, then into fourths, then each fourth into three equal parts; into how many equal parts is the whole line now divided? How many twelfths make one half of the whole? One fourth? One third? One sixth? Two sixths? Three sixths? Four sixths? Two thirds? Three fourths?

C. 1. The number 10 is already divided into two equal parts; what part of the ten is one of those parts? Two of the parts? Five of the parts? Six of the parts? Nine of the parts?

2. If you divide the number 10 into halves, how many tenths are there in one half? If you divide 10 into fifths, how many tenths are there in one fifth? How many tenths in two fifths? How many tenths in three fifths? In four fifths? In five fifths?

3. Draw a line and divide it into halves, then each half into five equal parts; into how many parts has the line been divided? What is the name of one of the parts? Three of the parts? Five of the parts? Seven of the parts?

4. How many tenths are equal to one fifth? Two fifths? Three fifths? Four fifths? Five fifths?

5. One half is equal to how many twentieths?

If you cannot tell otherwise, draw a line, and divide it first into halves, then into twentieths.

6. One fourth is how many twentieths? Two fourths is how many twentieths? Three fourths is how many twentieths?

7. One fifth is how many twentieths?

Draw a line, and divide it first into fifths, then into twentieths.

Two fifths is how many twentieths? Three fifths is how many twentieths? Four fifths is how many twentieths? Five fifths is how many twentieths?

8. Draw a line, and divide it into three equal parts; into how many parts will you divide each of the thirds, so that the whole line shall be divided into 15 equal parts? One third is how many fifteenths? How many fifteenths are equal to two thirds?

9. If you divide a line into five equal parts, how will you divide each of those parts, so that the whole line shall be divided into 15 equal parts? One fifth is how many fifteenths? Two fifths are how many fifteenths?

10. If you divide a line into two equal parts, how will you divide those parts so that the whole line shall be divided into fourteen equal parts? One half is how many fourteenths? Two halves are how many fourteenths?

11. Draw a line and divide it into seven equal parts; what will one of those parts be called? Two of the parts? How will you divide these parts so that the whole line shall be divided into fourteen equal parts? One seventh is how many fourteenths? Two sevenths are how many fourteenths? Three sevenths? Five sevenths? Six sevenths? Seven sevenths?

LESSON TWENTY-SEVENTH.

PARTS OF A NUMBER EXPRESSED IN PARTS OF A UNIT.

A. 1. What is one third of 12?

Draw as many equal lines as will represent one third of 12; calling each of these lines 1, divide it into three equal parts; each part is what part of 1? How many thirds of 1 do all the lines make? One third of 12 is equal to how many thirds of 1? One third of 12 is how many? Twelve thirds of 1 is how many?

2. What is one half of 6? How many halves of one is that equal to? One half of 6 is equal to how many halves of one? One half of 4 is how many halves of one?

3. One half of 3 is how many? One half of 3 is how many halves of one?

4. One half of 5 is how many? One half of 5 is how many halves of one?

5. One half of 7 is how many halves of one?

6. One half of 9 is how many? One half of 9 is how many halves of one?

7. One half of 10 is how many halves of one?

B. 1. One third of 2 is how many thirds of one?

The two lines *c* and *d* are divided into three equal parts, and one third of the two lines is cut off by the perpendicular line *r*. What is at the right hand of the line *r*, is one third of two; what part of one is it equal to?

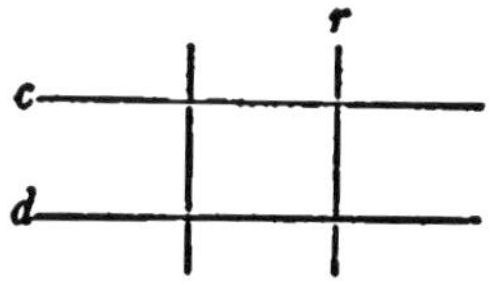

2. Two thirds of 2 is equal to what part of one?

3. One third of 4 is what part of one?

Draw 4 equal lines, and cut off one third of them; does it make more than one whole line—and if so, how much more?

4. Two thirds of 4 is what part of one?

5. One third of 5 is how many?

6. One third of 7 is how many?

7. Two thirds of 7 is how many? First find one third of 7.

8. One fifth of 2 is what part of one?

9. Two fifths of 2 is what part of one?

10. Three fifths of 2 is how many?

C. COLUMNS OF NUMBERS TO BE DIVIDED.

One sixth of	1	2	3	4	5	6
One fifth of	1	2	3	4	5	6
One fourth of	1	2	3	4	5	6
One third of	1	2	3	4	5	6
One half of	1	2	3	4	5	6

First Mode of Recitation.—Begin with the lowest line: "One half of 1 is one half; one half of 2 is one; one half of 3 is one and a half," &c. Then take the line above: "One third of 2," &c.

Second Mode.—Begin with the left-hand column: "One half of 1; one third of 1;" then, "One half of 2; one third of 2," &c. Then take the column of 3's.

---

1. How will you draw lines so as to show that one fifth of 4 is equal to four-fifths of one?

2. How will you draw lines to show that one sixth of 5 is five sixths of one?

3. How will you draw lines to show that one fourth of 3 is three fourths of one?

LESSON TWENTY-EIGHTH.

EXPRESSION OF PARTS BY FIGURES.

A. If we wish to express in figures *one half*, we write $\frac{1}{2}$: the figure below the line showing into how many equal parts the thing is divided; the figure above showing how many of those parts are taken.

If we divide a thing into 3 equal parts, we write 3 below the line, and we write above it a figure to show how many of those parts we take.

1. How would you express in figures one third? (Consider how many parts the thing has been divided into.) Two thirds? One fourth? Two fourths? Three fourths?

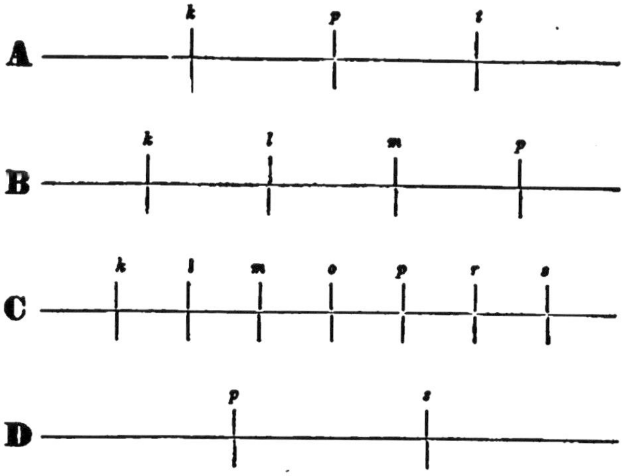

2. In the line A what part of the line is to the right of *t*? What part is to the left of *t*? What part is to the right of *p*? What part is to the left of *p*? What part is to the right of *k*? What part is to the left of *k*?

3. In the line B, how will you express in figures the two parts of the line as divided at *p*: first the right-hand part; second the left-hand part? How will you express the two parts as divided at *m*? As divided at *l*? As divided at *k*?

4. In the line C, how will you express the two parts as divided at *s*? As divided at *r*? As divided at *p*? As divided at *o*? As divided at *m*? At *l*? At *k*?

5. If the line A were divided into 8 equal parts, how many of those parts would there be at the right of *t*? How would you then express the part at the right of *t*? How will you express what is at the right of *t*, as it is divided in the book? Are these two expressions just equivalent to each other?

6. In the line A how will you express the part at the right of *p*? If the line were divided into 8 equal parts, how else could you express the part at the right of *p*? If the divisions at *t* and *k* were rubbed out, how would you then express the part at the right of *p*?

7. In the line D, how will you express the parts made by the division at *s*? If the line D were divided into 12 equal parts, how many of them would be on the right of *s*? How might you then express what is on the right of *s*?

8. How will you express the parts of the line D made by the division at *p*? How would you express those same parts if the whole line were divided into 12 equal parts?

B. 1. How will you divide a line on your slate so as to take $\frac{2}{3}$ of it?

2. How will you divide a line and show $\frac{1}{4}$ of it? $\frac{2}{4}$ of it? $\frac{3}{4}$ of it?

3. How will you divide a line and show $\frac{1}{5}$ of it? $\frac{2}{5}$? $\frac{3}{5}$? $\frac{4}{5}$?

4. How will you divide a line and show $\frac{1}{6}$ of it? $\frac{2}{6}$? $\frac{3}{6}$? $\frac{4}{6}$? $\frac{5}{6}$?

An expression in figures for something less than one, is called a Fraction. The figure showing how many equal parts the unit is divided into, is called the Denominator. The figure showing how many of those parts are taken, is called the Numerator.

5. What are the denominators of the fractions in question 2 above? What do they show? What are the numerators in the same fractions? What do they show?

6. Which is the greatest of the fractions in question 3? Which is the least? Which is the greatest fraction in question 4? Which is the next? Which is the smallest?

C. 1. Which is the greatest, $\frac{1}{8}$ or $\frac{1}{4}$? How many times does one of them contain the other?

Draw a line, and divide it into eighths and into fourths.

2. Which is the greatest, $\frac{1}{5}$ or $\frac{1}{10}$? How many times does one contain the other?

3. Which is the greatest, $\frac{1}{3}$ or $\frac{1}{6}$? How many times does one contain the other?

4. Which is the greatest, $\frac{1}{2}$ or $\frac{1}{6}$? $\frac{1}{3}$ or $\frac{1}{12}$? $\frac{1}{6}$ or $\frac{1}{12}$?

5. John had $\frac{1}{2}$ of a dollar, James $\frac{1}{4}$ of a dollar, and Henry $\frac{1}{8}$ of a dollar; how many $\frac{1}{8}$ of a dollar did they all have?

6. What is the sum of $\frac{1}{4}$ of a dollar, and $\frac{3}{8}$ of a dollar?

7. John spent $\frac{1}{2}$ of a dollar for a book, and $\frac{3}{8}$ of a dollar for a handkerchief; what part of a dollar did he spend for both?

8. William went to the store with $\frac{1}{2}$ of a dollar; after spending $\frac{1}{8}$ of a dollar, what part of a dollar had he left?

9. A man paid $\frac{1}{2}$ of a dollar for his dinner, and $\frac{3}{10}$ of a dollar for provender for his horse; what part of a dollar did he spend in all?

10. A man bought some articles at a store, and on giving a dollar in pay, received $\frac{1}{4}$ of a dollar, and $\frac{1}{8}$ of a dollar back; what part of a dollar did his purchase amount to?

LESSON TWENTY-NINTH.

ADDITION AND SUBTRACTION OF FRACTIONS.

A. *Fractions to be added.*

The sign +, called plus, signifies that the numbers between which it stands are to be added together; as 3+7, 3 and 7 added. The sign = signifies that the numbers before it are equal to those after it, as $3+7=10$, 3 + 7 equal 10.

A	B	C
$\frac{1}{2}+\frac{1}{4}$*	$\frac{1}{2}+\frac{1}{8}$	$\frac{1}{2}+\frac{1}{4}+\frac{1}{8}$
$\frac{1}{2}+\frac{2}{4}$	$\frac{1}{2}+\frac{3}{8}$	$\frac{1}{2}+\frac{3}{4}+\frac{1}{8}$
$\frac{1}{2}+\frac{3}{4}$	$\frac{1}{2}+\frac{5}{8}$	$\frac{1}{2}+\frac{3}{8}+\frac{1}{4}$
$\frac{1}{4}+\frac{1}{8}$	$\frac{1}{2}+\frac{7}{8}$	$\frac{1}{2}+\frac{5}{8}+\frac{1}{4}$
$\frac{2}{4}+\frac{1}{8}$	$\frac{1}{2}+\frac{2}{8}$	$\frac{1}{2}+\frac{7}{8}+\frac{1}{4}$
$\frac{3}{4}+\frac{1}{8}$	$\frac{1}{5}+\frac{3}{10}$	$\frac{1}{2}+\frac{5}{8}+\frac{3}{4}$
$\frac{1}{4}+\frac{3}{8}$	$\frac{4}{5}+\frac{1}{10}$	$\frac{1}{2}+\frac{7}{8}+\frac{3}{4}$

* Note Q.

B. *Add the first two Fractions, and from their Sum subtract the third.*

The sign −, called minus, signifies that the number after it is to be taken from the number before it.

A	B
$\frac{1}{3}+\frac{1}{4}-\frac{1}{6}$	$\frac{1}{3}+\frac{1}{8}-\frac{3}{8}$
$\frac{1}{2}+\frac{3}{4}-\frac{1}{8}$	$\frac{5}{6}+\frac{1}{4}-\frac{1}{2}$
$\frac{1}{3}+\frac{1}{4}-\frac{5}{6}$	$\frac{7}{8}+\frac{1}{2}-\frac{1}{8}$
$\frac{1}{2}+\frac{1}{8}-\frac{1}{4}$	$\frac{3}{8}+\frac{3}{4}-\frac{1}{2}$
$\frac{1}{4}+\frac{1}{8}-\frac{3}{8}$	$\frac{3}{8}+\frac{1}{4}-\frac{2}{8}$
$\frac{1}{8}+\frac{3}{4}-\frac{5}{8}$	$\frac{1}{8}+\frac{7}{8}-\frac{3}{4}$

C. 1. $\frac{1}{2}$ of a foot + $\frac{1}{3}$ of a foot + $\frac{1}{12}$ of a foot = how many $\frac{1}{12}$ of a foot?

2. $\frac{1}{3}$ of a foot + $\frac{1}{6}$ of a foot = how many $\frac{1}{12}$ of a foot?

3. $\frac{1}{4}$ of a foot + $\frac{2}{3}$ of a foot + $\frac{1}{6}$ of a foot = how many $\frac{1}{12}$ of a foot?

4. $\frac{1}{3}$ of a foot + $\frac{1}{4}$ of a foot − $\frac{1}{6}$ of a foot = how many $\frac{1}{12}$ of a foot?

5. $\frac{3}{4}$ of a foot + $\frac{1}{12}$ of a foot − $\frac{5}{12}$ of a foot = how many $\frac{1}{12}$ of a foot?

6. $\frac{2}{3}+\frac{1}{12}-\frac{5}{12}$ = how many $\frac{1}{12}$?

7. $\frac{1}{5}+\frac{3}{10}$ = how many $\frac{1}{10}$?

8. $\frac{2}{5}+\frac{3}{10}$ = how many $\frac{1}{10}$?

9. $\frac{2}{5}+\frac{4}{5}-\frac{7}{10}$ = how many $\frac{1}{10}$?

10. $\frac{4}{5}+\frac{3}{10}$ = how many $\frac{1}{10}$?

11. $\frac{3}{5}+\frac{7}{10}-\frac{2}{5}$ = how many $\frac{1}{10}$?

12. $\frac{1}{5}+\frac{3}{10}-\frac{1}{10}$ = how many $\frac{1}{10}$?

LESSON THIRTIETH.

MULTIPLICATION OF WHOLE NUMBERS AND FRACTIONS.

A. 1. A man is picking apples in a basket which holds $1\frac{1}{2}$ bushels; how many bushels does he pick if he fills the basket twice? How many if he fills it 3 times? If he fills it 4 times?

2. A carpenter is measuring a room with a rule $1\frac{1}{3}$ feet in length: the height of the room is 5 times the length of the stick; how many feet in height is it? The width of the room is 8 times the length of the stick; how many feet is it in width? The length of the room is 11 times the length of the stick; how many feet in length is it?

3. A shopkeeper in measuring cloth uses a stick 4 feet long; that is, $1\frac{1}{3}$ yards: he measures one piece 4 times the length of his stick; how many yards long is it? He measures another piece 6 times the length of his stick; how many yards long is it? A third piece is 9 times the length of his stick; what is its length in yards?

4. A man earns $1\frac{1}{4}$ dollars a day; how many dollars does he earn in 6 days? In 10 days? In 12 days? In 13 days? In 20 days?

5. If one bushel of wheat is worth $1\frac{1}{5}$ dollars, what will be the value of 6 bushels? Of 8 bushels? Of 10 bushels?

6. If a man earns $1\frac{1}{6}$ dollars in a day, how many dollars will he earn in 9 days? In 12 days? In 15 days? In 17 days?

7. If a bushel of grain lasts a family $1\frac{1}{7}$ weeks, how many weeks will 5 bushels last them? How many weeks will 7 bushels last them? 10 bushels? 12 bushels? 15 bushels?

B. Mixed Numbers to be multiplied.

10 times	$1\frac{1}{2}$	2	$2\frac{1}{2}$	3	$3\frac{1}{2}$	4	$4\frac{1}{2}$	5
9 times	$1\frac{1}{2}$	2	$2\frac{1}{2}$	3	$3\frac{1}{2}$	4	$4\frac{1}{2}$	5
8 times	$1\frac{1}{2}$	2	$2\frac{1}{2}$	3	$3\frac{1}{2}$	4	$4\frac{1}{2}$	5
7 times	$1\frac{1}{2}$	2	$2\frac{1}{2}$	3	$3\frac{1}{2}$	4	$4\frac{1}{2}$	5
6 times	$1\frac{1}{2}$	2	$2\frac{1}{2}$	3	$3\frac{1}{2}$	4	$4\frac{1}{2}$	5
5 times	$1\frac{1}{2}$	2	$2\frac{1}{2}$	3	$3\frac{1}{2}$	4	$4\frac{1}{2}$	5
4 times	$1\frac{1}{2}$	2	$2\frac{1}{2}$	3	$3\frac{1}{2}$	4	$4\frac{1}{2}$	5
3 times	$1\frac{1}{2}$	2	$2\frac{1}{2}$	3	$3\frac{1}{2}$	4	$4\frac{1}{2}$	5
2 times	$1\frac{1}{2}$	2	$2\frac{1}{2}$	3	$3\frac{1}{2}$	4	$4\frac{1}{2}$	5

First Mode of Recitation.—Begin with the column $1\frac{1}{2}$ at the bottom: "Two times $1\frac{1}{2}$, three times $1\frac{1}{2}$," &c. Then the column 2; then $2\frac{1}{2}$, and so on.

Second Mode.—Begin with the bottom line at the left, and proceed to the right. Then take the line above.

C. Mixed Numbers to be multiplied.

10 times	$1\frac{1}{3}$	$1\frac{2}{3}$	2	$2\frac{1}{3}$	$2\frac{2}{3}$	3	$3\frac{1}{3}$	$3\frac{2}{3}$	4	$4\frac{1}{3}$
9 times	$1\frac{1}{3}$	$1\frac{2}{3}$	2	$2\frac{1}{3}$	$2\frac{2}{3}$	3	$3\frac{1}{3}$	$3\frac{2}{3}$	4	$4\frac{1}{3}$
8 times	$1\frac{1}{3}$	$1\frac{2}{3}$	2	$2\frac{1}{3}$	$2\frac{2}{3}$	3	$3\frac{1}{3}$	$3\frac{2}{3}$	4	$4\frac{1}{3}$
7 times	$1\frac{1}{3}$	$1\frac{2}{3}$	2	$2\frac{1}{3}$	$2\frac{2}{3}$	3	$3\frac{1}{3}$	$3\frac{2}{3}$	4	$4\frac{1}{3}$
6 times	$1\frac{1}{3}$	$1\frac{2}{3}$	2	$2\frac{1}{3}$	$2\frac{2}{3}$	3	$3\frac{1}{3}$	$3\frac{2}{3}$	4	$4\frac{1}{3}$
5 times	$1\frac{1}{3}$	$1\frac{2}{3}$	2	$2\frac{1}{3}$	$2\frac{2}{3}$	3	$3\frac{1}{3}$	$3\frac{2}{3}$	4	$4\frac{1}{3}$
4 times	$1\frac{1}{3}$	$1\frac{2}{3}$	2	$2\frac{1}{3}$	$2\frac{2}{3}$	3	$3\frac{1}{3}$	$3\frac{2}{3}$	4	$4\frac{1}{3}$
3 times	$1\frac{1}{3}$	$1\frac{2}{3}$	2	$2\frac{1}{3}$	$2\frac{2}{3}$	3	$3\frac{1}{3}$	$3\frac{2}{3}$	4	$4\frac{1}{3}$
2 times	$1\frac{1}{3}$	$1\frac{2}{3}$	2	$2\frac{1}{3}$	$2\frac{2}{3}$	3	$3\frac{1}{3}$	$3\frac{2}{3}$	4	$4\frac{1}{3}$

LESSON THIRTY-FIRST.

FRACTIONS MULTIPLIED TOGETHER.

A. 1. A man bought $\frac{1}{2}$ of a barrel of flour, and sold $\frac{1}{3}$ of what he bought; what part of a barrel did he sell? What part of a barrel did he keep?

2. Draw a line, and divide it into halves; then divide each half into 3 equal parts: $\frac{1}{3}$ of $\frac{1}{2}$ is what part of the whole?

3. What part of a foot is $\frac{1}{3}$ of $\frac{1}{2}$ a foot?

4. One third of $\frac{1}{2}$ a dollar is what part of a dollar?

5. A man bought $\frac{1}{3}$ of a cord of wood, and gave away half of what he bought; what part of a cord did he give away?

6. Draw a line, and divide it into thirds; then divide one third into halves: $\frac{1}{2}$ of $\frac{1}{3}$ is what part of the whole?

7. $\frac{1}{2}$ of $\frac{2}{3}$ is what part of the whole?

8. Draw a line on the slate, and mark off $\frac{2}{3}$ of it; then take $\frac{1}{2}$ of that $\frac{2}{3}$, what fraction of the whole will it be?

Draw another line, and mark off $\frac{2}{3}$ of it; then take $\frac{1}{2}$ of one of those thirds, and then $\frac{1}{2}$ of the other, and add them together; what fraction will it be?

9. $\frac{1}{3}$ = how many sixths? How would you divide a line to get $\frac{1}{3}$ of it? How would you divide a line to get $\frac{3}{8}$ of it?

10. A man bought $\frac{1}{4}$ of a hundred weight of sugar, and sold half of it to his neighbor; what part of a hundred weight did his neighbor have? What is $\frac{1}{2}$ of $\frac{1}{4}$?

11. Draw a line, and mark off $\frac{3}{4}$ of it; how will you find $\frac{1}{2}$ of that $\frac{3}{4}$? What part of the whole line is it?

12. Two men own together $\frac{3}{4}$ of a ton of hay; on dividing it equally, what part of a ton does each one have?*

13. A man agrees to work a day for $\frac{3}{4}$ of a dollar; if he works only $\frac{1}{2}$ of a day, what part of a dollar ought he to receive?

14. When corn is worth $\frac{4}{5}$ of a dollar a bushel, what part of a dollar is 1 peck worth? What part of a dollar is $\frac{1}{2}$ of a peck worth?

* Note R.

15. What is $\frac{1}{2}$ of $\frac{1}{3}$? What is $\frac{1}{2}$ of $\frac{2}{3}$? What is $\frac{1}{2}$ of $\frac{3}{3}$?

16. If 1 dollar will buy 10 yards of sheeting, what part of a dollar will buy 1 yard? What part of a dollar will be the price of $\frac{1}{2}$ of a yard?

17. What is $\frac{1}{2}$ of $\frac{1}{10}$? $\frac{1}{2}$ of $\frac{2}{10}$ is how many $\frac{1}{20}$? $\frac{1}{2}$ of $\frac{2}{10}$ is how many $\frac{1}{10}$?

18. $\frac{1}{2}$ of $\frac{4}{10}$ is how many $\frac{1}{20}$? $\frac{1}{2}$ of $\frac{4}{10}$ is how many $\frac{1}{10}$?

19. One inch is $\frac{1}{12}$ of a foot; what part of a foot is $\frac{1}{2}$ of an inch? $\frac{1}{3}$ of an inch? $\frac{1}{4}$ of an inch?

20. $\frac{1}{3}$ of $\frac{1}{10}$ is what part of one whole?

Divide a line first into 10 equal parts; then divide the tenths each into 3 equal parts.

21. $\frac{1}{3}$ of $\frac{1}{5}$ is what part of one whole?

22. $\frac{1}{3}$ of $\frac{3}{5}$ is what part of one whole?

23. $\frac{1}{4}$ of $\frac{1}{5}$ of a dollar is what part of a dollar?

24. How will you divide a line so as to find $\frac{1}{4}$ of $\frac{3}{5}$ of it?

25. How will you divide a line so as to find $\frac{1}{3}$ of $\frac{3}{7}$ of it?

B. 1. What part of one week is one day? Two days? Three days? Four days?

2. $\frac{1}{2}$ of a day is $\frac{1}{2}$ of what part of a week? $\frac{1}{3}$ of a day is $\frac{1}{3}$ of what part of a week?

3. What part of a week is $\frac{1}{3}$ of a day? What part of a week is $\frac{2}{3}$ of a day?

4. How can you divide a line so as to show what fraction $\frac{1}{3}$ of $\frac{2}{7}$ is equal to?

5. $\frac{1}{3}$ of $\frac{3}{7}$ is how many $\frac{1}{21}$? How many $\frac{1}{7}$?

6. If a bar of iron weighs $\frac{1}{9}$ of a hundred weight, what part of a hundred weight will $\frac{1}{2}$ of the bar weigh? What part of a hundred weight will $\frac{1}{3}$ of it weigh?

7. What is $\frac{1}{2}$ of $\frac{3}{9}$? $\frac{1}{2}$ of $\frac{4}{9}$? $\frac{1}{2}$ of $\frac{5}{9}$?

8. Draw a line, and divide it into tenths; what part of the whole line is $\frac{1}{3}$ of $\frac{1}{10}$?

9. What is $\frac{1}{10}$ of $\frac{1}{3}$? How can you divide a line so as to show $\frac{1}{10}$ of $\frac{1}{3}$ of it?

10. What is $\frac{1}{10}$ of $\frac{2}{3}$? What is $\frac{1}{3}$ of $\frac{2}{10}$?

11. What part of a week is $\frac{1}{6}$ of a day? What part of a week is $\frac{5}{6}$ of a day?

12. What part of 4 weeks is 1 day? 3 days? 5 days?

13. What part of 2 bushels is 1 peck? 3 pecks?

14. What part of 3 weeks is 1 day? 5 days?

15. What part of 2 feet is 1 inch? 7 inches?

16. $\frac{1}{2}$ of a dollar is what part of 3 dollars? $\frac{1}{2}$ of a dollar is what part of 5 dollars?

17. What part of 2 gallons is 3 quarts? 5 quarts?

18. James has a pole 3 yards in length: he cuts off 2 feet from it; what part of the pole does he cut off?

19. A man agrees to work 5 weeks for a certain sum, working 6 days for a week: he works only 9 days; what part of the whole pay ought he to receive?

20. What part of 7 pounds is $1\frac{1}{2}$ pounds?

C. 1. From a piece of cloth $3\frac{1}{2}$ yards in length, how many caps can be made, each requiring $\frac{1}{2}$ of a yard of the cloth?

2. From a vessel containing $9\frac{1}{2}$ gallons, how many $\frac{1}{2}$ gallons can be drawn?

3. From a stick of wood $6\frac{1}{3}$ feet in length, how many blocks may be cut each $\frac{1}{3}$ of a foot long?

4. How many fourths of a hundred weight are there in $7\frac{3}{4}$ hundred weight?

5. Mr. A. pays away $5\frac{1}{2}$ dollars in wages to his hired man, giving him $\frac{3}{4}$ of a dollar a day; for how many days' labor does he pay him?

6. How many days will $6\frac{1}{2}$ pounds of bread last a man, if he uses $\frac{3}{4}$ of a pound each day?

7. How many $\frac{1}{15}$ are there in $\frac{4}{5}$?

8. How many $\frac{1}{10}$ are there in $\frac{3}{5}$?

9. How many $\frac{1}{20}$ are there in $\frac{3}{4}$?

10. How many $\frac{1}{18}$ are there in $\frac{4}{9}$?

D. 1. What is $\frac{2}{3}$ of $\frac{4}{5}$?

First find $\frac{1}{3}$ of $\frac{1}{5}$; then $\frac{1}{3}$ of $\frac{4}{5}$; then $\frac{2}{3}$ of $\frac{4}{5}$.

2. A boy having $\frac{3}{10}$ of a dollar, gave away $\frac{3}{4}$ of what he had; what part of a dollar did he give away?

Begin by finding $\frac{1}{4}$ of $\frac{1}{10}$.

3. How much is $\frac{2}{7}$ of $\frac{4}{9}$? First, what is $\frac{1}{7}$ of $\frac{1}{9}$?

4. How much is $\frac{3}{10}$ of $\frac{4}{5}$?

5. A man having $\frac{3}{4}$ of a cord of wood, sold $\frac{2}{5}$ of what he had; what part of a cord did he sell?

6. A man owning $\frac{4}{5}$ of a share in a Bank, sold $\frac{2}{3}$ of what he owned; what part of a share did he sell?

7. $\frac{2}{7}$ of $\frac{4}{9}$ of a dollar is what part of a dollar?

8. $\frac{4}{5}$ of $\frac{2}{3}$ of a cord of wood is what part of a cord?

9. What is $\frac{3}{4}$ of $\frac{7}{8}$? $\frac{3}{4}$ of $\frac{5}{6}$?

10. What is $\frac{3}{5}$ of $\frac{4}{5}$? $\frac{2}{3}$ of $\frac{4}{7}$?

LESSON THIRTY-SECOND.

CHANGE OF FORM IN FRACTIONS.

A. 1. Draw a line, and divide it into 2 equal parts; write the fraction expressing one half of the line: if you had divided the line into 4 equal parts, what would the denominator have been? What must the numerator be, over that denominator, to signify one half?

2. What fraction will signify one half, if the denominator of the fraction is 6? If it is 8? If it is 10?

3. What fraction will signify one half if the numerator is 3? If it is 4? If it is 5? If it is 7? If it is 9?

4. Examine the two fractions $\frac{1}{2}$ and $\frac{3}{6}$, whose values are the same; what is the first numerator multiplied by to make the second numerator? What is the first denominator multiplied by to make the second denominator? Have both terms therefore been multiplied by the same number?

5. Multiply both terms of the fraction $\frac{1}{2}$ by 4, what fraction does it give? Is its value the same as before?

Multiply both terms by 5. Is the value changed? Multiply both terms by 6. By 7. By 8. Is the value still the same?

6. If I take the fraction $\frac{1}{2}$, and multiply the denominator by some number, without multiplying the numerator, shall I alter the value of the fraction? What must I do to the numerator to bring its value to what it was before?

7. If you multiply the numerator of $\frac{1}{2}$ by any number, and do not multiply the denominator, will it change the value of the fraction? What must be done to the denominator to make the value of the fraction the same as it was before?

8. If you multiply the denominator of $\frac{1}{5}$ by 3, and do not wish to alter the value of the fraction, what more must you do? What must you do to preserve the value of the fraction, if you multiply the numerator by 4? The denominator by 3? The denominator by 10? The numerator by 9? The numerator by any number whatever? The denominator by any number whatever?

9. A man bought $\frac{2}{3}$ of a cord of wood at one time, and $\frac{3}{5}$ of a cord at another; how much did he buy in all?

As we cannot multiply either denominator by any number that will make it agree with the other, we will multiply both terms of the first fraction by the denominator of the second; what fraction will that give? Is its value the same as $\frac{2}{3}$?

Next we will multiply both terms of the second fraction by the denominator of the first; what fraction will that give? Is its value the same as $\frac{3}{5}$? You can now add the fractions without further aid.

10. What part of a dollar is $\frac{1}{2}$ of a dollar and $\frac{1}{3}$ of a dollar? Proceed as in the last example.

11. What part of a dollar is $\frac{1}{2}$ of a dollar and $\frac{3}{5}$ of a dollar?

12. Add $\frac{1}{2}$ and $\frac{3}{5}$. Add $\frac{1}{3}$ and $\frac{4}{5}$.
13. Add $\frac{1}{3}$ and $\frac{1}{4}$. Add $\frac{1}{3}$ and $\frac{3}{4}$.
14. Add $\frac{1}{4}$ and $\frac{2}{3}$. Add $\frac{3}{4}$ and $\frac{2}{3}$.
15. Add $\frac{1}{3}$ and $\frac{1}{5}$. Add $\frac{1}{5}$ and $\frac{2}{5}$.
16. Add $\frac{2}{3}$ and $\frac{1}{5}$. Add $\frac{2}{3}$ and $\frac{4}{5}$.
17. Add $\frac{1}{4}$ and $\frac{2}{5}$. Add $\frac{3}{4}$ and $\frac{3}{5}$.

18. Add $\frac{1}{3}$ and $\frac{4}{7}$. Add $\frac{1}{2}$ and $\frac{4}{7}$.
19. Add $\frac{1}{3}$ and $\frac{3}{8}$. Add $\frac{1}{3}$ and $\frac{5}{6}$.
20. Add $\frac{1}{4}$ and $\frac{3}{5}$. Add $\frac{3}{4}$ and $\frac{4}{5}$.

B. When two fractions are changed in form, as in the preceding questions, they are said to be reduced to a common denominator; that is, they are so changed that they both have the same denominator.

1. From $2\frac{2}{3}$ gallons of water how many bottles can be filled, each containing $\frac{3}{10}$ of a gallon?

First find how many thirds there are in $2\frac{2}{3}$; then reduce the two fractions to a common denominator, and the question will be, how many times is $\frac{9}{30}$ contained in $\frac{80}{30}$?

2. How many times is $\frac{3}{7}$ of a hundred weight contained in $2\frac{1}{3}$ hundred weight?

3. How many sticks $1\frac{1}{5}$ feet long can be cut from a pole $9\frac{1}{3}$ feet in length?

4. How many times is $1\frac{1}{3}$ contained in $7\frac{1}{4}$?

5. How many times is $2\frac{1}{5}$ contained in $10\frac{1}{2}$?

6. How many times is $3\frac{1}{2}$ contained in $13\frac{2}{5}$?

7. How many buckets of water, each containing $2\frac{1}{4}$ gallons, will it take to fill a cask containing $10\frac{1}{3}$ gallons?

8. If from a cask containing $7\frac{1}{2}$ gallons, $2\frac{1}{3}$ gallons be drawn, how much will remain?

9. If from a load of hay, weighing $12\frac{1}{2}$ hundred, $3\frac{1}{7}$ hundred be taken, how much will remain?

10. From a pole $11\frac{1}{4}$ feet long, $2\frac{1}{7}$ feet were taken, how many feet long was the remainder?

11. A man has $3\frac{1}{4}$ dollars, and pays away $2\frac{3}{5}$ dollars, how much will he have remaining?

12. What is the amount of $4\frac{1}{2}$ dollars and $3\frac{3}{4}$ dollars added together?

LESSON THIRTY-THIRD.

MULTIPLICATION—LINEAR MEASURE—MEASURES OF CAPACITY.

A. *Multiplication Table.*

Once	1	2	3	4	5	6	7	8	9	10	11	12
Twice	1	2	3	4	5	6	7	8	9	10	11	12
3 times	1	2	3	4	5	6	7	8	9	10	11	12
4 times	1	2	3	4	5	6	7	8	9	10	11	12
5 times	1	2	3	4	5	6	7	8	9	10	11	12
6 times	1	2	3	4	5	6	7	8	9	10	11	12
7 times	1	2	3	4	5	6	7	8	9	10	11	12
8 times	1	2	3	4	5	6	7	8	9	10	11	12
9 times	1	2	3	4	5	6	7	8	9	10	11	12
10 times	1	2	3	4	5	6	7	8	9	10	11	12
11 times	1	2	3	4	5	6	7	8	9	10	11	12
12 times	1	2	3	4	5	6	7	8	9	10	11	12

First Mode of Recitation.—Begin with the left-hand column at the top: "Once 1, twice 1," &c. Then take the column of 2's: "Once 2, twice 2," &c.

Second Mode.—Beginning at the top, take the lines horizontally from the left: "Once 1, once 2," &c. Then "Twice 1, twice 2," &c.

Third Mode.—Name the multiples or products only: first, in perpendicular order; then, horizontally.

Products to be divided.

4	6	8	10	12	14	15	16	18	20	22
24	25	26	28	30	33	35	36	40	42	44
45	48	49	50	55	60	63	64	66	70	72
77	80	84	90	96	100	108	110	121	132	144

First Mode of Recitation.—Name the number first, and then name the factors which produce it.

Second Mode.—Looking at the number, name at once the factors which produce it.

When a number is produced by either of two pairs of factors, (as 12, which is 3 times 4, also 6 times 2,) both pairs of factors should be named; if there are more than two, all of them should be named.

B. Table of Linear Measure.

12 inches make	- - - -	1 foot.
3 feet	- - - - - -	1 yard.
$5\frac{1}{2}$ yards = $16\frac{1}{2}$ feet	- - -	1 rod.
40 rods	- - - - - -	1 furlong.
8 furlongs	- - - - -	1 mile.

---

1. How many inches are there in $1\frac{1}{3}$ feet? In 2 feet? In 3 feet?

2. How many inches are there in $2\frac{1}{4}$ feet? In $3\frac{3}{4}$ feet? In $4\frac{1}{2}$ feet?

3. There is a stick $2\frac{1}{3}$ feet in length; if you cut off $\frac{1}{2}$ of a foot at one end and $\frac{1}{3}$ of a foot at the other, and then cut the remainder into 2 equal parts, how many inches long will one of the parts be?

4. There is a stick 2 feet long; if it is cut into 3 equal pieces, how many inches long will one of the pieces be? If it is cut into 8 equal pieces, how many inches long will each of the pieces be? If it is cut into 4 equal parts, how many inches long will one of the parts be?

5. There are two sticks; one is $3\frac{1}{4}$ feet in length, the other $2\frac{3}{4}$ feet in length; how many inches longer is the one than the other?

6. There are 12 lead pencils in a bunch, each 5 inches long; if they are placed in a straight line, end to end, how many feet long will the line be?

7. There are 10 sticks, each $\frac{3}{4}$ of a foot in length; if they are placed end to end, what will be the length of the whole?

8. How many feet are there in $3\frac{1}{3}$ yards? In $4\frac{1}{2}$ yards? In 7 yards?

9. There is a pole 20 feet in length; if $3\frac{1}{2}$ feet are cut off from it, how many yards in length will the remainder be?

10. There is a pole 13 feet long; if $1\frac{1}{3}$ yards be cut off, how many yards long will the remainder be?

11. There is a line $3\frac{1}{2}$ yards in length; how much must be added to it to make it 15 feet long?

12. If you add $3\frac{1}{2}$ yards and $4\frac{1}{3}$ yards together, how many feet in length will it be?

13. If a man in walking steps 3 feet each step, how many steps will he take in walking 2 rods? How many steps will he take in walking 3 rods? How many in walking 4 rods?

14. If a boy steps 2 feet at each step, how many steps will he take in walking 1 rod? In walking 2 rods? 3 rods? 4 rods?

15. How many furlongs are there in $2\frac{1}{2}$ miles? In $4\frac{1}{4}$ miles?

16. A. and B. set out from the same place and walk in the same direction: A. walks $3\frac{1}{2}$ miles, B. walks $2\frac{7}{8}$ miles; how many furlongs apart are they then?

17. A. and B. set out from the same place: A. walks east $3\frac{1}{4}$ miles, B. walks west $2\frac{3}{8}$ miles; how many miles are they apart then? How many furlongs?

18. *How many rods are there in $\frac{1}{2}$ of a furlong? In $\frac{1}{4}$ of a furlong? In $\frac{1}{5}$ of a furlong? In $\frac{3}{4}$ of a furlong? In $\frac{4}{5}$ of a furlong?

* Note 8.

19. How many furlongs are there in $6\frac{1}{4}$ miles? In $8\frac{3}{4}$ miles?

20. If a man travels $5\frac{1}{2}$ miles from home, and then returns $4\frac{3}{4}$ miles, how many furlongs from home will he then be?

C. TABLE OF DRY MEASURE.

For measuring grain, fruit, &c.

2 pints make - - - - - -	1 quart.
4 quarts - - - - - - -	1 gallon.
8 quarts = 2 gallons - - -	1 peck.
4 pecks - - - - - - -	1 bushel.

The pint, the quart, and the gallon are used both for dry articles and for liquids; but the dry measure, in this country, contains a little more than the liquid measure. In England the capacity of the measure is the same for both.

---

1. A man bought a peck of plums and sold 2 quarts and 1 pint of them, how many pints had he left?

2. How many pints are there in $3\frac{1}{2}$ quarts? In $5\frac{1}{2}$ quarts?

3. A man having a basket full of peaches, containing 3 pecks, sold one peck of them to one person, and a peck and a half to another; how many quarts had he left?

4. In one basket there are 3 pecks of peaches, in another half as many; how many quarts more than a bushel are there in both baskets?

5. There are 12 baskets, each containing 3 pecks; how many bushels do they all contain?

6. There are 12 bags of wheat, each containing $1\frac{1}{2}$ bushels; how many bushels do they all contain?

7. There is a bin containing $4\frac{3}{4}$ bushels of rye; how many bags, each containing 3 pecks, can be filled from it?

8. How many quarts are there in $\frac{1}{8}$ of a bushel? In $\frac{3}{4}$ of a bushel? In $1\frac{1}{4}$ bushels? In $1\frac{3}{8}$ bushels?

9. Mr. B. carries a bushel of corn to mill: the miller takes $\frac{1}{16}$ of it as his pay for grinding; how many quarts are ground for Mr. B. to carry home?

10. If a family consume 3 quarts of meal in a day, how many days will 3 pecks of meal last them?

11. If 5 bushels of wheat last a family 8 weeks, how many quarts will last them one week?

12. A horse consumes 7 bushels of oats in 4 weeks, how many bushels will he consume in one week?

13. If a family consume 2 quarts of meal in a day, in how many days will they consume a bushel?

14. In how many days will a family consume a bushel of meal, if they consume each day 5 quarts? If they consume 4 quarts? If they consume 6 quarts?

15. How many gallons are there in $3\frac{1}{2}$ bushels? In $4\frac{1}{4}$ bushels? In $2\frac{7}{8}$ bushels?

16. How many baskets, containing $1\frac{1}{2}$ pecks, can be filled from a heap of apples containing $7\frac{1}{2}$ bushels?

17. How many half pecks are there in $2\frac{1}{4}$ bushels? In $3\frac{1}{8}$ bushels?

18. There are two bags: the first contains $\frac{1}{2}+\frac{1}{4}+\frac{1}{8}$ of a bushel, the second contains $\frac{1}{2}$ of a bushel and 13 quarts more; which bag contains the most?

D. Table of Liquid Measure.

Wine Measure.

4 gills make - - - - - -	1 pint.
2 pints - - - - - -	1 quart.
4 quarts - - - - -	1 gallon.
$31\frac{1}{2}$ gallons - - - - -	1 barrel.

This measure is used for all liquids, except beer and milk. For beer and milk the measures have the same names, but they are somewhat larger. There are 36 gallons in a barrel of beer.*

---

1. How many gills are there in $3\frac{1}{2}$ pints? In $2\frac{1}{4}$ pints? In $2\frac{3}{4}$ pints?

2. How many gills are there in 1 quart? In $2\frac{1}{2}$ quarts? In $3\frac{1}{4}$ quarts?

* Note T.

3. How many pints are there in 1 gallon? In $\frac{1}{2}$ of a gallon? In $\frac{1}{4}$ of a gallon?

4. How many pints are there in $2\frac{1}{2}$ gallons? In $4\frac{1}{4}$ gallons? In $5\frac{3}{4}$ gallons?

5. If from a vessel, containing $2\frac{1}{2}$ gallons, 5 quarts are drawn out, how many quarts will remain? How many pints? How many gills?

6. One half of 3 gallons is how many pints? How many gills?

7. From a vessel containing 10 quarts, how many bottles can be filled each containing 3 pints?

8. From a barrel containing $31\frac{1}{2}$ gallons, how many bottles can be filled each containing 2 quarts?

9. How many half pints are there in 7 gallons?

10. What part of $1\frac{1}{2}$ gallons is 1 pint? 3 pints? 5 pints?

LESSON THIRTY-FOURTH.

MONEY—WEIGHTS—CLOTH MEASURE.

A. TABLE OF FEDERAL MONEY.

Used in the United States.

10 mills make - - - - - -	1 cent.
10 cents - - - - - -	1 dime.
10 dimes - - - - - -	1 dollar.
10 dollars - - - - -	1 eagle.

1. How many cents are there in 2 dimes? In 3 dimes? In 5 dimes? In 7 dimes? In 8 dimes? In 9 dimes?

2. How many cents are there in $2\frac{1}{2}$ dimes? In $4\frac{1}{2}$ dimes?

3. How many dimes are there in 40 cents? In 60 cents? In 70 cents? In 30 cents? In 45 cents? In 25 cents?

4. How many mills are there in half of a cent? In $2\frac{1}{2}$ cents? In 4 cents? In $3\frac{1}{2}$ cents? In 7 cents?

5. How many dimes are there in 2 dollars? In 4 dollars? In $2\frac{1}{2}$ dollars? In $6\frac{1}{2}$ dollars?

6. How many cents are there in 1 dollar? In $\frac{1}{2}$ of a dollar? In $\frac{1}{4}$ of a dollar?

7. How many cents are there in $\frac{1}{5}$ of a dollar? In $\frac{1}{10}$ of a dollar? In $\frac{3}{10}$ of a dollar? In $\frac{7}{10}$ of a dollar?

8. How many dollars are there in $2\frac{1}{2}$ eagles? In $3\frac{1}{4}$ eagles? In $6\frac{1}{2}$ eagles? In $4\frac{3}{4}$ eagles?

9. John has $\frac{1}{4}$ of a dollar, and James has $\frac{2}{5}$ of a dollar; which of them has the most, and how much?

10. A man having received 4 dimes for some apples, and 3 dimes for some peaches, paid away half a dollar of it for flour; how many cents had he left?

11. John has $\frac{1}{2}$ of a dollar in one hand, and $2\frac{1}{2}$ dimes in the other; how many fourths of a dollar has he in both?

12. A man bought 7 pounds of coffee for 10 cents a pound: he gave the grocer a dollar bill; how many cents ought he to receive back in change?

13. A boy sold 5 measures of plums for 6 cents a measure; how many dimes did they all come to?

14. A man bought 4 melons for 7 cents apiece, and 2 quarts of plums for 6 cents a quart: he gave half a dollar in pay; how many cents should he receive back?

15. A gentleman boards 3 days at an hotel, at $1\frac{1}{2}$ dollars a day: he gives a five dollar bill in pay; how much ought he to receive back?

16. A lady gave a dollar bill in pay for $6\frac{1}{2}$ yards of muslin, at 10 cents a yard; how many cents should she receive back?

17. What part of a dime is 3 cents? 5 cents? 8 cents?

18. How many mills are there in 4 cents? In $5\frac{1}{2}$ cents? In $\frac{1}{2}$ of a dime? In $\frac{1}{4}$ of a dime? In $\frac{3}{4}$ of a dime?

19. James has 7 dimes; Henry has $\frac{1}{2}$ of a dollar, and $\frac{1}{4}$ of a dollar: which has the most, and how much?

20. William has $2\frac{1}{2}$ dimes; Charles has $\frac{4}{10}$ of a dollar: which has the most, and how much?

21. How many cents are there in 7 half dimes? In 8 half dimes? In 9 half dimes?

22. Charles gave 7 half dimes in pay for 4 quarts of nuts at 8 cents a quart: how many cents should he receive back?

B. TABLE OF STERLING MONEY.

*The Money of Great Britain.**

4 farthings make - - -	1 penny.
12 pence - - - - -	1 shilling.
20 shillings - - - - -	1 pound.

---

1. How many farthings are there in 3 pence? In $4\frac{1}{2}$ pence? In $5\frac{3}{4}$ pence? In $10\frac{1}{2}$ pence?

2. How many farthings are there in 1 shilling? In half a shilling? In $2\frac{1}{4}$ shillings? In $1\frac{1}{2}$ shillings?

3. How many pence are there in $2\frac{3}{4}$ shillings? In 5 shillings? In $3\frac{1}{4}$ shillings? In 4 shillings and 6 pence?

4. A lady bought 3 yards of riband for 1 shilling and 6 pence a yard, and gave 8 shillings in pay; how many shillings and pence should she receive back?

5. How many shillings are there in 2 pounds? In 3 pounds? In half a pound? In one fourth of a pound?

6. How many shillings are there in $1\frac{1}{4}$ pounds? In $2\frac{1}{2}$ pounds?

7. How many shillings are there in $3\frac{1}{2}$ pounds? In $4\frac{1}{4}$ pounds?

8. If $12\frac{1}{2}$ cents make 1 shilling, how many cents are there in 2 shillings? In 3 shillings? In 4 shillings? In 5 shillings? In 6 shillings? In 7 shillings? In 8 shillings?

9. If $16\frac{2}{3}$ cents make 1 shilling, how many cents will then be in 2 shillings? In 3 shillings? In 6 shillings? In 4 shillings? In 5 shillings?

* NOTE.—This money was used in this country when the states were provinces of Great Britain: and it is still used here to some extent. The value of the denominations in this country varies in the different states. In the New England states the value of a shilling is $16\frac{2}{3}$ cents; in New York it is $12\frac{1}{2}$ cents. In England it is about 22 cents.

10. If there are 8 shillings in 1 dollar, how many cents will there be in 4 shillings? In 2 shillings? In 1 shilling?

11. If 6 shillings make 1 dollar, how many cents will there be in 3 shillings? In 1 shilling?

C. Table of Avoirdupois Weight.

Used in weighing hay, grain, meat, groceries, &c.

16 drams make	-	1 ounce.
16 ounces	- -	1 pound.
25 pounds	- -	1 net quarter of a hundred.
28 pounds	- -	1 gross quarter of a hundred.
4 quarters	- -	1 hundred weight.
20 hundred	- -	1 ton.

---

1. How many drams in $2\frac{1}{2}$ ounces? In 3 ounces? In $1\frac{3}{4}$ ounces? In 4 ounces?

2. How many ounces in $\frac{1}{2}$ a pound? In $\frac{3}{4}$ of a pound? In $4\frac{1}{4}$ pounds?

3. At 8 cents a pound what will be the price of $3\frac{1}{2}$ pounds of sugar? Of $4\frac{1}{4}$ pounds? Of 5 pounds?

4. In net weight how many pounds are in 2 quarters? In 3 quarters? In 4 quarters?

5. In gross weight how many pounds are there in 2 quarters? In 3 quarters? In 4 quarters?

6. How many hundred weight are there in half a ton? How many hundred weight in one fourth of a ton?

7. What part of a ton is 1 hundred weight? 2 hundred weight? 4 hundred weight? 10 hundred weight?

8. A man having $1\frac{1}{2}$ tons of hay, sells one half of it at the rate of 12 dollars a ton; how many dollars ought he to receive?

9. A teamster has $\frac{1}{2}$ a ton of loading in one place, and $\frac{3}{4}$ of a ton in another; how many hundred weight are there in both places?

10. If hay is worth 10 dollars a ton, what is 1 hundred weight worth?

D. Table of Troy Weight.

Used in weighing gold and silver.

24 grains make	- - -	1 pennyweight.
20 pennyweights	- - -	1 ounce.*
12 ounces	- - - -	1 pound.

1. How many grains are there in half a pennyweight? How many grains in $\frac{2}{3}$ of a pennyweight?

2. One third and one fourth of a pennyweight are how many grains?

3. One sixth and one eighth of a pennyweight are how many grains?

4. How many pennyweights are there in $\frac{1}{2}$ of an ounce? In $2\frac{3}{4}$ ounces? In $3\frac{1}{4}$ ounces?

5. How many grains are there in $\frac{1}{3}$ of an ounce?

6. How many pennyweights are there in $\frac{1}{4}$ of a pound? How many pennyweights are there in $\frac{1}{6}$ of a pound?

E. Apothecaries' Weight.

Used in dealing out Medicines.

20 grains make	- - - -	1 scruple.
3 scruples	- - - - -	1 dram.
8 drams	- - - - -	1 ounce.
12 ounces	- - - - -	1 pound.

1. How many grains make $\frac{1}{2}$ a scruple? $\frac{1}{4}$ of a scruple? $\frac{1}{5}$ of a scruple?

2. How many grains are there in 2 scruples? In 1 dram? In $1\frac{1}{2}$ drams? In 2 drams?

3. How many grains make $\frac{1}{2}$ of a dram? $\frac{1}{4}$ of a dram?

4. How many drams are there in $\frac{1}{2}$ an ounce? In $\frac{1}{4}$ of an ounce? In $\frac{3}{4}$ of an ounce?

5. How many scruples are there in $\frac{1}{2}$ an ounce? In $\frac{1}{4}$ of an ounce? In $1\frac{1}{2}$ ounces? In 2 ounces?

* The ounce Troy is a little heavier than the ounce Avoirdupois; the pound Troy, of 12 ounces, is somewhat lighter than the pound Avoirdupois.

F. Table of Cloth Measure.

$2\frac{1}{4}$ inches make - - - -	1 nail.
4 nails - - - - -	1 quarter.
4 quarters - - - -	1 yard.
3 quarters - - - -	1 ell Flemish.
5 quarters - - - -	1 ell English.
6 quarters - - - -	1 ell French.

1. How many inches are there in 2 nails? In 3 nails?

2. How many nails are there in $\frac{1}{2}$ a yard? In 1 yard?

3. How many quarters are there in 2 yards? In $2\frac{1}{4}$ yards? In $2\frac{3}{4}$ yards? In $4\frac{1}{2}$ yards?

4. How many ells Flemish are there in 3 yards? In 4 yards?

5. How many inches are there in 1 quarter of a yard? In 3 quarters?

6. If you have a riband 1 yard long, and cut off 1 ell Flemish from it, how many inches long will the remainder be?

7. How many inches longer is an ell French than an ell Flemish?

8. Charles has a line measuring an ell French, an ell English, a yard, and an ell Flemish, in length; William has a line measuring $4\frac{1}{2}$ yards in length: whose line is the longest, and how much?

9. If you had a yard stick, how many inches must you cut off of it so as to leave it an ell Flemish in length?

10. If you have a stick an ell French in length, and cut it into 2 equal parts, how many inches long will one of the parts be?

11. How many half yards are equal to 3 ells French?

12. How many yards are equal to 4 ells French?

13. What will $2\frac{1}{4}$ yards of muslin come to at 15 cents a yard?

14. What will $6\frac{3}{4}$ yards of cloth come to at 4 dollars a yard?

15. What will 7 yards of cloth cost at $4\frac{1}{2}$ dollars a yard?

16. What will be the cost of $\frac{3}{4}$ of a yard of cassimere at 90 cents a yard?

LESSON THIRTY-FIFTH.

ADDITION AND MULTIPLICATION.

A. *Columns for Practice in Addition.*

A	B	C	D	E	F	G	H	I	J
5	4	9	1	7	6	9	7	4	1
4	1	7	4	3	8	6	8	6	9
4	7	8	4	9	5	5	3	2	8
9	6	6	6	4	9	3	4	7	2
6	1	3	9	0	1	8	5	9	4
7	6	5	7	7	6	4	6	2	6
3	9	4	2	8	3	2	3	5	3
8	7	9	3	6	7	7	4	6	7
6	5	9	4	5	8	7	6	3	7
9	4	3	8	3	8	8	7	6	3
7	3	7	6	9	4	4	8	5	6
3	7	6	7	8	9	9	9	4	4
8	9	8	9	4	5	1	7	2	6
6	7	1	4	8	6	6	3	4	4
9	6	9	3	6	7	8	4	5	5
5	5	7	5	0	3	4	6	3	5
4	8	7	6	0	4	2	7	3	5
9	3	3	8	9	4	7	2	4	5

First Mode of Recitation.—Begin with column J: "5 and 5 are ten, and 5 are fifteen," &c.

Second Mode.—Name the sums made by addition, thus: "Column J—five, ten, fifteen," &c.

To vary the exercise, sometimes one scholar should add a whole column; again, each may add a single figure; or, finally, the whole class may add together.

To vary the exercise still further, the teacher may name some number, and the class may add the required column to it. This will prevent the wearisome recurrence of the same numbers.

B. *Exercises in Multiplication.*

A	B	C
2134312	6914324	146792
2	3	5

D	E	F
6943285	4379645	9437654
6	8	7

G	H	J
7963428	5964321	7964389
34	86	246

First Mode of Recitation.—"Example A: Twice 2 are four, twice 1 are two, twice 3 are six," &c.

Second Mode.—Multiply silently, and name the figures to be set down, thus—"Example A: Four, two, six," &c.

If the multiplication of two figures gives a product greater than ten, first add aloud the number carried; thus—"Example B: Three times 4 are twelve; three times 2 are six, and *one are seven.*" *Second Mode:* Multiply and carry silently, naming only the figures to be set down; thus—"Example B: Two, seven, nine, two, four, seven, twenty."

PART FIFTH.

ANALYSIS—GENERALIZATION—SQUARE MEASURE—CONSTRUCTION OF FIGURES.

LESSON THIRTY-SIXTH.

ANALYSIS—GENERALIZATION.

A. 1. John has 18 cents, which is once and a half as many as James has; how many has James?*

2. Henry's age is 10 years, which is once and a fourth the age of William; how old is William?

3. Charles and James have some apples: one third of Charles's number is 4, and the whole of his is once and a fifth as many as James has; how many has James?

4. Says Peter, "One third of my marbles and two more are nine;" how many had he?

5. Sarah is 14 years old, which is once and two fifths the age of Mary; what is Mary's age?

6. William having 16 cents, spent a part of it, when he found that what he had left was one third as much as he had spent; how many cents had he spent?

7. There are two bars of lead, both together weighing 20 pounds: the larger weighs four times as much as the smaller; what does the smaller weigh?

8. The age of John and that of James, added together, is 27 years, and John's age is 3 years more than half of James's age; how old is each of them?

9. One fourth of one third of a certain sum is 4 dollars; if you subtract 8 dollars from the sum what will one fifth of the remainder be?

10. The ages of Charles and Sarah, added together, are 11 years, and the age of Sarah is one year less than half the age of Charles; what is the age of each of them?

* Note U.

11. There are 13 plums on a plate, some of them blue, and the rest white; if you should put two more white ones on the plate, the blue ones would then be two thirds of the whole; how many are there of each kind?

12. Charles has one half as many cents as William; he spends one cent and then he has one third as many as William; how many had they each at first?

13. If a boy lose two thirds of one half of his money, and has nine cents left, how many cents had he at first?

14. Frank and Joseph have each the same number of cents; Frank spends one third of his, and Joseph one fourth of his, and then Joseph has two cents more than Frank; how many cents had they at first?

15. A man, having sold one third of all his peaches, had $1\frac{1}{3}$ bushels left; how many had he at first?

16. If you take away two apples from a plate, and that leaves three-fourths as many as there were before, how many were there on the plate at first?

17. Mr. A. on a journey spends two dollars the first day; and one half of what he had left, the second day; and then found he had one third as much money as when he set out; how much had he when he set out?

18. Mr. B. on a journey spends two dollars the first day; and one half of what he had left, the second day; and then found he had one fourth as much money, as when he set out; how much had he when he set out?

19. A boy has some marbles; he loses first, two, and then loses one third of the remainder, and has left half as many as he had at first; how many had he at first?

20. What number is that of which two thirds is 3 more than one half?

B. Questions in Generalization.

1. If one yard of cloth cost a certain number of cents, how can you find what a given number of yards of the same cloth would cost?

2. If a man earn a certain number of shillings in one day, how can you find how much he will earn in a given number of days? In what denomination will the answer be: and why? In what denomination was the answer to the preceding question?

3. If you know the cost of a certain number of bushels of wheat, how can you find the price of one bushel? Give an example.

4. If you know the cost of a certain number of cords of wood, how can you find the cost of one cord?

5. If you know the price of a ton of hay, how can you find the price of half a ton? How can you find the price of any given part of a ton?

6. If you know the price of a ton of hay, how can you find the price of any given number of hundred weight?

7. If you know the cost of building one yard of wall, how can you find the cost of building one rod of wall?

8. If you know the cost of building one rod of wall, how will you find the cost of building two yards of wall?

9. If you know the price of one bushel of rye, how will you find the price of $3\frac{1}{2}$ pecks of rye? Give an example.

10. If you know the price of board for one week, how will you find the cost of board for any given number of weeks, and any given part of a week over?

11. A. and B. buy a load of wheat together for a certain sum, agreeing to divide it afterwards, and to pay according to what each one should have; on dividing it, A. takes one half as much as B.; what part of the price of the whole ought each to pay?

12. A. and B. purchase a lot of wood together for a certain sum, and on dividing it, A. has two thirds as much as B.; what part of the price of the whole ought each to pay?

13. If one barrel of wheat, containing $3\frac{1}{4}$ bushels, cost a certain sum, how will you find the cost of one bushel of the wheat?

LESSON THIRTY-SEVENTH.

SQUARE MEASURE.

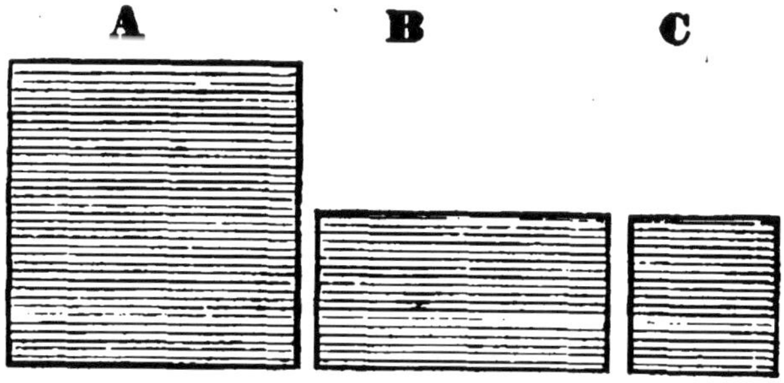

A. 1. The figure at A is one inch long, and one inch wide; how long is the figure at B? How wide is it? How long is the figure at C? How wide is it?

2. How many bounding lines has the figure at A? Are these lines all of the same length?

3. How many bounding lines has the figure at B? What is the length of the horizontal lines? What is the length of the perpendicular lines?

4. Is the figure at C shaped like the figure at A, or like that at B? In what respect is it like one; not like the other?

5. Is the figure at C nearest in size to the figure at B, or to that at A? How many figures like that at C would be equal to one like that at B? How many like that at B would equal the figure at A? How many like that at C would equal that at A?

The figure at A is a square inch. It is a square because its sides are all equal and its corners are square.

The figure at B is a rectangle. Its opposite sides are equal, and its corners are square.

Draw on your slate a figure like that at A, as follows. Draw first the lower horizontal line, one inch long. Next, at the right-hand point of this line, draw a perpendicular line, one inch long. Then draw a like perpendicular from the left-hand point. Finally, draw a horizontal line from the top of one perpendicular to the top of the other.

Remember to call the first line you draw the *base;* the second, the *right perpendicular;* the third, the *left perpendicular;* and the fourth, the *top line.* Draw now a figure 2 inches long, and 1 inch wide. Be careful to make the corners square.

6. How long is the base? The right perpendicular? The left perpendicular? The top line? How many square inches does it contain?

7. If you draw a rectangle 3 inches long, and one inch wide, how many square inches will it contain?

8. If you draw a rectangle 4 inches long, and one inch wide, how many square inches will it contain? How many square inches would it contain if it was 5 inches long, and one inch wide? How many, if it was 6 inches long and one inch wide?

9. Draw a figure 2 inches long and 2 inches wide; how many square inches does it contain?

10. Draw a rectangle 3 inches long, and 2 inches wide; how many square inches does it contain? What is the length of its base? Its perpendiculars? Its top line?

11. How many square inches would a rectangle contain, if it was 4 inches long, and 2 inches wide? If it was 5 inches long, and 2 inches wide? If 5 inches long, and 3 inches wide? If 5 inches long, and 4 inches wide?

12. How many square inches is there in a rectangle 6 inches long, and 2 inches wide? 6 inches long, and 3 inches wide? 6 inches long, and 4 inches wide?

13. How many square inches are there in a square foot? Consider how many inches long, and how many inches wide it is.

14. How many square feet are there in a square yard? Consider how many feet long, and how many feet wide it is.

15. How many square feet are there in a board four feet long, and one foot wide? In a board 7 feet long, and one foot wide?

16. How many square yards are there in a piece of cloth one yard wide, and 5 yards long? In a web one yard wide, and 15 yards long?

17. How many square yards of cloth are there in a web 2 yards wide, and 5 yards long? In a web 2 yards wide, and 12 yards long?

18. The page on which I am writing is 10 inches long, and 8 inches wide; how many square inches are there in it?

19. A little boy is reading a book, a page of which is 5 inches long, and 3 inches wide; how many square inches does it contain?

20. A page of note paper is 6 inches long, and 4 inches wide; how many square inches does it contain?

B. 1. If you cut a piece of paper 2 inches long and half an inch wide, how can you divide it and place the parts so as to make just one square inch?

2. How many square inches are there in a rectangle 4 inches long and half an inch wide? In a rectangle 6 inches long and half an inch wide? 5 inches long and half an inch wide?

3. Draw a rectangle 2 inches long and $1\frac{1}{2}$ inches wide; how many square inches does it contain?

4. How many square inches in a rectangle, if it is 4 inches long and $1\frac{1}{2}$ inches wide? If 6 inches long, and $2\frac{1}{2}$ inches wide?

5. How many yards of cloth $\frac{1}{2}$ a yard wide will be equal to 1 square yard? To 2 square yards? To 3 square yards?

6. How many yards of cloth $\frac{1}{3}$ of a yard wide will be equal to 1 square yard? To 2 square yards?

7. There is a strip of board 3 inches wide and 12 inches long; how many such placed side by side would make a square foot?

8. If a piece of board is 4 inches wide, how many feet in length must it be to contain a square foot?

9. A certain writing-desk is 4 feet long, and $2\frac{1}{4}$ feet wide; how many square feet does it contain?

10. How many square feet are there in a board 2 feet wide and $4\frac{1}{2}$ feet in length?

LESSON THIRTY-EIGHTH.

CONSTRUCTION OF FIGURES.

In drawing the following figures, the first line is always a horizontal, or level line, which will be called the base. In drawing a perpendicular to the base, remember to have it lean neither to the right nor left.

The letter B. will stand for base; P. for perpendicular; *r. p.* for the right-hand end or point of the base; *l. p.* for the left-hand point; and *m. p.* for its middle point. To obtain this last you must divide the base into two equal parts, and mark the middle point. R. P. stands for right-hand perpendicular; L. P. for left-hand perpendicular.

Fig. 1. Draw B. (that is, a base line) 3 inches in length. From *r. p.* draw P.=$\frac{1}{3}$ of B. From *l. p.* draw P.=$\frac{1}{3}$ of B. Draw a line from the top of L. P. to the top of R. P. How many square inches does the figure contain?

Observe, every line drawn should be a straight line.

Fig. 2. Draw B. 3 inches in length. From *r. p.* draw P.=$\frac{2}{3}$ of B. From *l. p.* draw P.=$\frac{2}{3}$ of B. Draw a line from the top of L. P. to the top of R. P. How many square inches does the figure contain?

Fig. 3. Draw B. 3 inches in length. From *r. p.* draw P.=B. Draw a line from *l. p.* to the top of P. Can you divide the figure so as to tell how many square inches it contains?

Fig. 4. Draw B. any length you choose. From *r. p.* draw P.=$\frac{1}{4}$ of B. From *l. p.* draw P.=$\frac{1}{4}$ of B. Draw a line from the top of L. P. to the top of R. P. How many squares can you divide the figure into? How can you divide it into 2 rectangular figures, each twice as long as it is wide?

Fig. 5. Draw B. of any length. Draw from *r. p.* P.=$\frac{3}{4}$ of B. From *l. p.* draw P.=$\frac{3}{4}$ of B. Draw a line from the top of L. P. to the top of R. P. How can you divide the figure into 3 rectangles, each four times as long as it is wide? How can you divide the figure into 4 rectangles, each 3 times as long as it is wide?

Fig. 6. Draw B. 2 inches in length. Through *m. p.* draw P.=B, half above B, and half below. Draw lines from the two ends of P. to the two ends of B. Can you find how many square inches the figure contains?

Fig. 7. Draw B. Draw from *r. p.* P.=½ of B. From *l. p.* draw P.=½ of B. Draw a line from top of L. P. to top of R. P. Draw a line from *l. p.* to top of R. P. Draw a line from top of L. P. to *r. p.* From *m. p.* draw P.=R.P. Into how many parts is the figure now divided? Are they all equal? If not, how many are there of the largest size equal to each other? How many smaller ones equal to each other?

Fig. 8. Draw B. 2 inches in length. From *r. p.* draw P.=½ of B. From *l. p.* draw P.=½ of B. From *m. p.* draw P.=B. Draw a line from top of L. P. to top of R. P. Draw lines from top of the middle P. to top of R. P. and top of L. P. How many square inches are there in the whole?

NOTES TO THE TEACHER.

A. When the word Two is spoken, every one should look in the book to find the line of two dots. The same attention should be given when any other number is called. To aid in this, there should be a little pause after the first numerical word.

B. When more than two numbers are added, be careful to pause at each numerical word, and let the class follow the teacher with the answer at every step; thus—*Teacher.* "One—and two?" *Class.* "Three." *Teacher.* "And three?" *Class.* "Six."—Be careful that every eye is fixed on the teacher.

Lesson Second.—Lesson First does not exhaust the combinations in Addition as far as the Table furnishes the elements. It does not go beyond what will give the sum of *eight*, leaving the combinations of 2, 3, and 4 = 9; and of 1, 2, 3, and 4 = 10, for separate lessons afterwards. Before proceeding to them, it is important that the elements already given be made still more familiar, by changing the operation from Addition to Subtraction.

C. Let the Class give the second part the moment the Teacher has given the first.

A pleasant variation of this exercise is to divide the Class into two parts, letting one part open their books and read the first part of the number, and the other portion of the Class give the second part.

Another useful exercise in Addition is to make a number of marks on the blackboard. Let the Class count and see how many there are; then, with a writing-book or some convenient thing, cover a part of the marks, requiring the Class to tell, by looking at those in sight, how many are covered.

D. As the idea of local value has no place in these exercises, let the pupil take those dots together which are grouped together for the eye.

This addition should be practised till it can be performed as quickly as the child can speak. It should be practised both upwards and downwards; sometimes naming each group as it occurs before adding it to the sum already in mind; sometimes naming only the sums. The first column added in the first mode, would be recited as follows: "One and two are three, and one are four, and three are seven." In the second mode it would be one, three, four, seven. To enliven the exercise, it should be sometimes transferred to the board, and gone through by the whole class together.

E. The Class should not attempt this exercise until they are perfect in those of a like kind upon the lower numbers, 6, 7, and 8.

F. Do not attempt here to explain how the division can be made and be equal. It is sufficient for the present object that the child should see that it is not equal, as made in the question. In studying this lesson the children should be encouraged to use the slate.

G. Be careful to say "*not equal*," rather than *unequal*. The first form of expression being entirely negative, stimulates the pupil's mind to seize with avidity the affirmative expression as soon as the question presents the occasion for it.

H. The word half is here introduced without being defined. The reason is that every child able to begin the study of numbers knows the meaning of one half. His experience has taught him both the idea and the term, a hundred times. I wish therefore, by all means, to avail myself of that knowledge; and the teacher should in no case encumber the term *half*, at this point, with any words of explanation.

J. Let the answer be given strictly; not allowing the pupil to say that three is one half of five, because it is as great as one half.

K. If any one in the Class so far anticipates the division of the unit as to give one and a half as the half of three, let him be told that the question is, Can he divide three into halves without dividing one? If no one takes the above step, the division of the unit should not be suggested to the Class at this time. Let them come firmly against the difficulty and be stopped by it. Help will come in due time.

L. It is safe to presume that the child can count so as to answer the first questions asked here. In describing the line let the child tell first, how many stars—then, how many dots. If he counts, be careful that he counts the stars first, and then begins anew to count the dots. In this way will the mental process unfailingly fix in the pupil's mind the composition of the compound numerical word, four—teen, fif—teen, six—teen, &c.

If there is any hesitation, be careful not to prompt the Class, but let every eye be fixed on the Teacher, while he pronounces again *Six—teen*; and hold the pupils to this point till the true answer is given.

In training pupils to a ready command of the composite words between ten and twenty, it is important to put the smaller number first, as *four and ten*, not *ten and four*; because this is the order in which the compound word presents the parts. Having learned to associate the two parts as thus given with the compound word, the order of the parts may then be changed, and the child will soon answer the question with equal readiness in either form, four and ten, or ten and four.

M. If the Teacher will faithfully train his pupils in these and the other tables of a similar kind, he will need no word in commendation of the plan to assure him of its peculiar fitness to form the habit of rapid calculation. In the first place, it is an exercise in Addition, the most important of all the operations in Numbers. Second, the attractive form of the lesson to the eye does much to secure the attention of each one in the Class to every step in the recitation. Third, it conducts the mind up by successive steps to the number to be divided, so that when the sum is found there is no danger that the pupil will have a mere word in his mind, without an idea. Fourth, it lightens the labor of the Teacher, as he has no questions to ask, and only general directions to give.

N. This simple variation of linear measure is the first instance of denominate numbers introduced in the book; because it is one of the easiest, and, what is more important, it admits of convenient illustration. Let the illustration be given on the board.

O. It is better to throw the pupil on his own reflection than to dictate to him what name to give the part here described. A recurrence to the names he has already learned to give to parts obtained by division will suggest what the name should be in this case. The same observation is applicable to similar questions that follow.

P. After the Class are able to add these columns promptly in the way here directed, they may be allowed to write and add them on the slate. They will hardly need a word of instruction if first made familiar with the exercise orally.

Q. If the pupils show any want of readiness in this exercise, let them be put to the work of dividing a line on the slate or board, as indicated by the question in hand. This exercise should be repeated till the process can be performed by the pupils as rapidly as they can speak; giving each step of the process aloud.

R. If any pupil divides the $\frac{3}{4}$ of the line into two equal parts, and says he thus obtains one and a half fourths, $\frac{1\frac{1}{2}}{4}$, let him be told that he gives a perfectly correct answer, but not so convenient in form as is desirable. To make the expression more simple, let him begin by dividing one of the fourths, then another, &c.; and add the results. The remark made above may be extended to all fractions when the numerator is not divisible by the required divisor. One half of $\frac{5}{7}$ is $\frac{2\frac{1}{2}}{7}$, or $\frac{5}{14}$; either answer is correct, but the last more convenient.

S. Pupils should early be taught to estimate distances in feet, rods, and furlongs. The first step is the measurement of distances by a line or pole. The second step is to estimate distances, and then to test the correctness of the estimate by measurement.

T. The omission of the higher liquid measures, tierce, hogshead, &c., is intentional. They vary in size, and seldom conform to the capacities assigned them in Tables. In strictness of language, neither these larger casks nor barrels are measures at all. From the nature of their construction they cannot be measures. They are only convenient receptacles for holding and conveying liquids.

U. Once and a half James's number is three halves of James's number; if three halves is 18, one half is one third of 18. In the following questions be careful to explain the process fully.

Made in United States
North Haven, CT
04 November 2026

21766933R00054